Sculpting Air

A Whole-Person Approach to Songwriting

Time and a Place Publishing

SCULPTING AIR - A WHOLE-PERSON APPROACH TO SONGWRITING
Written by Robert Walsh
Contributions by Jason Plume and Victoria Banks
Design by Valéry Goulet
Edited by Patricia Crowe

ISBN: 978-1-7753654-0-2 *Paperback*
978-1-7753654-1-9 *Ebook*

www.robertwalsh.ca

Thank You,

MacEwan University, songwriters and contributors Jason Blume and Victoria Banks, graphic designer Valéry Goulet, and my far-smarter-than-me editor and friend Patricia Crowe.

The colleagues and friends who responded to my call for suggestions, thoughts and opinions about what is important as I planned this book, namely: Alexis Normand, Charles Cozens, Rob Heath, Neil MacDonald, Joel Lavoie, Colleen Rae, Daniel ROA, Brendan Lyons, Moe Clark, Jeffrey Straker, Thom Bennett, France Lavasseur-Ouimet, Shawn Soucy, Stephen Maguire, Nathalie Ladouceur, Nathen Aswell, Stewart MacDougall, Charlie Austin, T-Bone Blaszko, and my long-time collaborator Andrea Menard. Tamara Cable for proof-reading and making some great saves. Alix Bean for passing the torch. The many students, artists and co-writers who have schooled me.

My wife, Rhonda Trodd, who continues to inspire and encourage me.

MacEwan
UNIVERSITY

Contents

Introduction

A good many books on songwriting are available from some excellent songwriters, and I will reference many of them in this book. Some are by hit makers, others by pedagogues and producers; each voice offers a different angle of entry to what is a multi-faceted creative pursuit. Now I add my voice to the subject. In so doing, I hope the reader will find practical information they can use that addresses the how-to's of songwriting, and find solutions to challenges around creativity, process and self-doubt. My writing on the subject has been coloured by the belief that songwriting calls our entire being to show up and get involved, and this "whole-person" approach is woven into the fabric of this book.

I come to songwriting as a musician with an extensive career writing and performing a wide variety of music in an assortment of places – from arenas, theatres and concert halls to cocktail parties and empty bars – and as an artist who has released many albums under my own name or as a collaborator in various projects, writing in English and French. I have written for myself, with others and for others, for theatre, film, big band, symphony orchestra, and for commissioned events and family occasions. Every song has taught me something. I've signed record deals, lost record deals, worked with famous people and should-be-famous people, and all along I've made a living in what my colleague Daniel ROA refers to as "the real music business." No blockbuster hits to set me up for retirement, but steady work and a great life making music that has had an impact on peoples' lives and garnered me a place amongst some rather exceptional peers. This book is largely informed by two bodies of experience. The first draws from the act of songwriting itself, something I've done for more than 40 years, writing in a wide variety of styles for every band I was a part of; for special projects; and for many solo artists. The work I've done as a producer has also had a great influence on how I see songwriting.

The second body of experience draws on the 20 plus years I've spent working with aspiring songwriters, leading workshops, developing a high school music program offered throughout Alberta that uses songwriting as its core method of instruction, and teaching the Songwriting course at MacEwan University in Edmonton.

When it comes to songwriting, I don't believe there are really any hard and fast rules. As John Braheny explains in his seminal book *The Craft and Business of Songwriting*, it's more about adopting guiding principles. Some of these principles depend on style and current trends; others, the more important ones, are grounded in deeper human values and an honest search for truth and beauty in art. I believe this search, and the offering of our findings to others, is the real work of songwriters.

A View From The Writer's Room – Philosophy And Perspective

"A genius is the one most like himself."

Thelonius Monk

It's ironic that the path to originality starts with learning to mimic others and acquiring universal skills necessary to express your individuality. What I hope to do in this book is shine some light down that path, and offer ideas and approaches to help you explore it.

I contend that all musicians should study songwriting simply because it'll improve their own understanding of music. Most musicians contribute their talents in the arena of the song – be it as singers, players, producers or arrangers – and spend their careers interpreting or adding their voices to the work done by songwriters. With song such a predominant form of music, it makes sense for anyone working with it to understand what goes into songwriting, even if it's not their main focus.

As a Canadian musician, I write and perform in English and French. In Western Canada where I live, French is a minority language. I've noticed that, whenever recording a song in French, the better musicians have made a point of finding out what the song is about before laying down their tracks. These players want to be sure to get the emotional lay of the land in order to respond musically to the song's needs. They also attune themselves to the elements of melody, dynamics and structure to ensure their efforts complement the song. A good grasp of song is necessary to get to this level.

With song playing such a pivotal role in music making, I find it hard to understand why so few post-secondary institutions offer songwriting as a core subject. I tip my hat to the ones who do, and to any organization that provides the opportunity for people to become songwriting students. And I reach out to my fellow musicians who choose this field of study, no matter where they find themselves on the continuum in terms of education, experience or age. For most of us, it's a life-long pursuit.

Songs are short stories, not novels. Videos, not movies. The small canvas. They are also not poetry, as I'll discuss later. Songs demand brevity, concision and the management of energy and thought. Songwriting also exacts a most difficult and challenging resource – courage. It asks of its writers to be authentic, and the root of authenticity is a willingness to take risks, say what you actually mean and mine the self that's seeking expression.

Finding Your Voice

Our beliefs form our worldview and make us express ourselves as we do. So any song you write will serve as a snapshot of how you're feeling and what you're thinking at a given time. We're all works in progress, and evolving people are willing to accept their beliefs may be wrong, undeveloped or incomplete. Curiosity and self-questioning are key habits for songwriters to acquire, even though the answers they reveal might change over time.

Exploring the themes of your life, all lives, saying what matters, revealing our humanity in all its colours is the role of the songwriter. Our work has the power to unite, heal, celebrate, protest, denigrate, accuse, evoke love, refute love, champion faith, refute faith, mourn, cajole, amuse, captivate and make us sing, dance, cry and yell.

Listeners, really interested only in authenticity, don't seek out the latest singer who sounds just like another singer. They want the original. They also don't care about perfect. As listeners, we're quick to forgive imperfection if the end result is beauty, truth or connection. Art requires risk, and the possibility of failure acts as fuel, giving power to action and heightening the experience. Faults and missteps are the price to pay for creativity. But it's a small price because art trumps perfection every time.

Does the world need another love song? Yes – it needs your love song. Writers have only so many themes to work from, but it's the unique essence each one of us brings to our work that makes new expressions of old themes interesting and relevant. For writing to feel genuine, we need to harness this essence. Shutting out the voice of the critic is paramount.

On Criticism and Managing Self-Doubt

The subject of what to do with criticism – both internal and external – is of great interest to me. At times, its destructive force has had a direct impact on me, and I've seen just how debilitating it can be for other artists as well. At its least harmful, it can lead to writer's block, disillusionment and the desire to quit; and at its worst, it can push people to addiction, mental unwellness and even suicide. Ultimately, we have to own our reactions to criticism, and we alone determine its effect on us, even if it feels unjust and crazy-making. When we see all criticism, positive and negative, for what it is – other people's thoughts – we can embrace the futility of trying to control it. This can lead to a healthy detachment that empowers you to cherry-pick what helps and leave aside the rest.

Author Wayne Dyer used to tell a story about how he received two letters on the same day about one of his books. The first correspondent wrote to say it was the worst book he had ever read and he regretted wasting his money on it. The second wrote to thank Dyer for writing one of the best books he'd ever read, one that had changed his life. In response, Dyer sent each writer a copy of the other's letter, a copy of his latest book and a note with one line: "You might be right."

Creative criticism – the kind we use to examine our own work and make necessary changes – can be extremely positive if we learn how to harness the internal critic's voice. If we adopt the attitude that there's always a better idea around the corner, it's easier to let go of the less worthy ones and not take any of it personally. This is even more important when working with a collaborator. Nothing will shut down a writing session more quickly than a precious or insecure attitude. When done with care and respect, and a belief you and your partner have the capacity to dig deeper, honest criticism moves creative work forward.

Severe internal criticism is the result of perfectionism, which is based in fear. This can only lead to self-doubt, and this negative spiral must not be allowed to continue. Sometimes it's spurred on by a devastating external critique like a bad review, a humiliating comment or being rejected for something. And sometimes it's triggered by the shame of not being famous in an industry where name recognition is equated with success.

Rejection is a part of any creative endeavour, and it has happened over and over to the best songwriters. I've devoted some time to criticism and negativity here in as much as they touch the lives of most songwriters, but a deeper examination may be necessary for any writer who is really struggling. For now, here are a few ideas that may help you cope with criticism and negativity:

It's simply none of my business. Other people's opinions, the level of success I attain – none of it is my business. My job is to create the best music I can and try to bring it to an audience. I'll do my best, but I can't be responsible for the outcome or for anybody else's reaction. That's entirely their business.

I can't really believe my own thoughts. Can I ever really know I'm 100% right? Can I know anybody else is? I remember a gig I did when I was sure the conductor hated what I was playing, and I was getting really bummed out about it. He took me aside at a rehearsal, and my heart started to race as I was sure he was going to fire me. To my shock, however, he told me he loved what I was doing and asked for my contact information! I try to remember this when I perceive things as terrible. This also means I must be willing to let go of the thought that something is amazing. If I can do this, too, then I become free to simply create what I think is best at the time, and live with the possibility that change may be necessary at some point. "You might be right" is a good motto that allows others their opinions while leaving you the freedom to do as you please.

Some other thoughts that might be helpful:

Don't put the pressure of being great on your writing. Showing up and doing your best is enough.

Don't put the pressure of earning your living on your writing. This might be too much to impose on your Muse. There's no shame in supporting yourself in other ways. It'll probably teach you something and provide inspiration for material.

Be on purpose. Serve your creative self. Write for the sake of writing. This is a constructive and positive act, and it helps everybody, even if they don't know it.

Writer's block occurs when the ego and the inner critic have the loudest voice. It's good to break the pattern and stop the loops of self-doubt by taking action. But try something new (perhaps you've also exhausted your usual writing patterns). Start with a groove, or lyrics or story first. Begin with the first line, or the chorus. Explore new keys, new chords, map out the form first, the story first, write the shape/contour of the melody before you sing it, pick a different time signature, find a co-writer, write for somebody else (for real or "in the style of"), etc. Study a favourite song and try writing a response to it. Or borrow a few things you can adapt – form, melodic contour, rhyme scheme, basic groove – and write your own tune. Shake it up!

Write a song to specifically work on a part of your game that needs to develop. For instance, if you've never written a story song with strong characters before, try it. Assemble as many tools in your toolkit as possible. To quote singer-songwriter Daniel ROA, "talent mixed with a wide skill set creates fulfillment AND a paycheque!"

Be aware there are avenues within what ROA calls "the real music industry," where "songwriters can find meaningful and paying work without trying to fit a mould." What he's getting at is that lots of unsigned artists are getting paid for their music – from live performances, non-hit radio, film, television, commercials, theatre and other outlets. And persistence pays off.

One more comment from ROA: **"Just keep going.** Over the years, one of the most important things for me to share is simply my love for the craft of songwriting. Playing with language, meaning, melody, harmony, rhythm, sounds ... all of those elements, are what ultimately create something to share, something with an emotional impact, something beautiful. Once shared, songs take on a life of their own, and that in itself is a pretty amazing transformation for what began with a simple spark of inspiration."

This should be a labour of love. And love is to be shared. Right?

Victoria's Secrets

Victoria Banks is an Ontario-born singer-songwriter making her living as both a recording artist and a staff songwriter in Nashville. When I told her I was writing a book, I asked her to put together some thoughts on songwriting. Being the great songwriter she is, what I got back was straight to the point, full of imagery, concise and memorable. I think you should put all her thoughts together, laminate them and carry them around like one of those mini-books found in the self-help section of your bookstore. Here is the first of three installments of Victoria's Secrets:

Listen to a ton of music. All different genres, Listen to the structure. Figure out why a song hits you the way it does. What is it about the song that hooks you in?

Learn the rules. Learn the generally accepted rules for how to structure songs within your genre or specialty. And then learn how to break them. Don't be afraid to try new things. Sometimes it doesn't work ... but sometimes it's just different enough to catch people's attention.

Write about everything. Keep a "hook book" and/or a bunch of voice memos, and keep track of potential song ideas. They could be phrases you hear in passing ... something on TV ... a passing verse lyric in a song that could be a whole song itself. They could be in books, on movie screens, on Facebook comment lists .... They're everywhere! Train yourself to walk around with your antennae tuned for the next idea. If you're not vigilant, you'll miss them.

Be specific. Put specific, colourful language in your songs. Why just say "losing you hurts," when you can say "losing you is like a shard of glass to the vein"? Give listeners something to visualize, and don't settle for generalizations unless you have to. Make every lyrical line of a song fight for its right to exist.

Learn to collaborate. As uncomfortable and awkward as it can be if you are an introverted songwriter, learning to collaborate is crucial. Not only does it challenge you and stretch your boundaries artistically, it also helps you become part of a team. When one person in the team makes a new contact or has some success, everyone benefits. Look at it like diversifying in a mutual fund – it's your best chance at being a part of something successful.

Victoria Banks has been nominated for 11 Canadian Country Music Association (CCMA) Awards and was named CCMA Female Artist of the Year and Songwriter of the Year in 2010. She has been labeled "one of the best songwriters in the business" by Nashville's Music Row Magazine.

In addition to releasing 3 albums and touring with artists from Reba to Wynonna, Victoria - who hails from Muskoka, Canada - has had an illustrious career as a songwriter, penning ASCAP, SOCAN, CCMA and Covenant-award-winning songs for over 50 artists. Her cuts include Jessica Simpson's Billboard record- breaking single "Come on Over", Sara Evans' hit "Saints & Angels" & duet "Can't Stop Loving You" (with Isaac Slade of the band The Fray), Johnny Reid's CCMA Song of the Year "Dance With Me", and many more.

On Creativity

According to Albert Einstein, creativity is intelligence having fun. So songwriting should be fun, right? In my experience, it is (although it often feels that way only after the fact). But it's also work, and for some people the idea of expressing their creative side can be downright scary.

Creativity Is Us

I'd like to dispel any notion that creativity is the sole domain of artists, and that you should be a little crazy and a touch irresponsible to be truly creative. Don't buy into this anachronistic stereotype.
Most successful musicians are highly disciplined and many are excellent entrepreneurs.

We humans are nothing but creative. Every decision, every act – how you smile, dress, drive, cook, show kindness, animosity, love – is creative because the possibilities are endless, and the choices we make create every moment of our lives. In fact, our creative skills are so great we can even create other lives.

Creativity is our greatest gift. It's what we're about.

Artists are often seen as particularly creative. But the only difference is that artists, engaged in a field where new work is constantly being forged, learn to nurture their creativity to the point where they can count on it.

Still, it takes grit. In my experience, some level of fear is a frequent companion for anyone leading a creative life, and efforts to eradicate fear rarely work. What does seem to work is when we allow fear to be part of the process, but don't permit it to have a voice in decision-making. With this approach, we let go of any notion of attaining the impossible goal of fearlessness, and replace it with achievable acts of bravery. Small victories lead to larger ones, and the habit of creativity develops.

Creativity thrives when it goes side by side with self-development. This is where the interplay between Intellect and Emotion, Craftsmanship and Inspiration, Organization and Intuition starts.

As for the Muse itself, who can say where it comes from? It's an age-old mystery artists probably will never solve. Just embrace it and invite it in. Over time I've come to trust that it will show up, as have many other artists whose livelihoods depend on it. And while the Muse's flash of creativity is the real-world definition of magic, it's also a stumbling block for those writers who feel that first idea is the best idea and to tamper with what they've channeled is blasphemy.

On the other end of the spectrum is the equally powerful workhorse of Intellect. This is the often-maligned organizer of thought, evaluator of ideas and voice of reason that so many artists see as the antithesis of creativity and want so desperately to reject. Songwriting involves the blending of magic (inspiration and expression) and industry (analysis and re-writing), and the key is to access both the Muse and the Intellect.

Conceptualists vs. Experimentalists

The economist and art lover David Galenson put forward a theory about creativity after examining the lives of visual artists, poets, novelists, filmmakers and musicians. As a songwriter, I find the most intriguing aspect of his theory is the observation that one camp of creators, whom he calls the Conceptualists, burst open with creativity at a young age, armed with clear direction, purpose and articulation, and a strategy for accomplishing their vision. Galenson offers Pablo Picasso as a prime example of a Conceptualist.

In contrast are the Experimentalists, whose creative journeys take many twists and turns and often leave creators feeling dissatisfied and their work unfinished. Galenson cites Paul Cézanne as a classic Experimentalist whose slow-moving genius is the opposite of Picasso's accelerated creativity. Cézanne was known to work on four different versions of the same idea simultaneously, frequently trashing his work to start again – he once made a portrait subject return for 100 sittings. Experimentalists are often unsure about, and frustrated with, their work, and it can take years, even a lifetime in Cézanne's case, to figure things out.

We all create differently because we are different, and the authenticity that comes with embracing our individuality is what makes art beautiful and valuable. Maybe you're more Picasso than Cézanne or vice versa. Either way, it doesn't matter, because songwriting's not about process, it's about creating art. And art is about communication.

The songwriter's main creative tools for communication are, of course, music and lyrics, and each one is a discipline worthy of study. To be a consistently effective songwriter, there are no shortcuts to putting in the time necessary to learn how to use these tools. However, you don't need to be a master musician to be a great songwriter, and there are no post-secondary degrees offered that I'm aware of for lyric writing.

Curiosity

The fundamental starting point for self-expression and creativity is curiosity. Curiosity about the first tool, music, can lead you to learn what's important – whether through credited programs, private study, learning online, or by picking the brains of established musicians. The information is there to be absorbed. The deeper the understanding of music history, technique and theory, the more options you'll have, and the broader your palette will be. How far you choose to go in your learning will be determined by your passion for the craft and the strength of your curiosity.

When it comes to lyric writing, there are far fewer formal avenues of study. However, many books, blogs and websites are devoted to the craft. Like learning music, your depth of study depends on your own ambition. However, the need for curiosity might be even greater for lyric writing than music. I'll discuss various approaches to lyric writing further in the book, but none of them will be worth much if the writer doesn't come to the table with a healthy inquisitiveness about the human condition. It's this innate curiosity about people, the world, life, that fuels the songwriter's imagination and leads to a point of view seeking expression. Our willingness to pay attention, expand, learn and wonder is directly related to our creativity as songwriters, and this is a muscle we can develop.

Sometimes our biggest creative block is the voice of our inner critic. When we control this voice, it can be a great ally, but left unchecked it will shut you down every time. There is a time for analysis and self-criticism in the process of songwriting (as I will discuss later), but the focus needs to remain on the work itself, and not on our self-worth. The finest songwriters have moments of being terrible songwriters, and I have yet to meet any pros who haven't written some pretty awful songs along the way. The biggest paradox in all of this is the fact that listeners often react favourably to the flaws we want to disguise. And it's the very willingness to expose our most honest selves and be vulnerable that will lead to being truly authentic.

For some aspiring songwriters, accessing creativity is emotionally charged because people or events have actively discouraged or suppressed creative expression. Author Julia Cameron (*The Artist's Way*) considers such people "recovering creatives," for whom finding a sense of safety in self-expression is a necessary first step. We all suffer from self-doubt and fear of expressing ourselves to some degree, and I find it helps to remember that creativity is not something for others, but is, in fact, our birthright.

So claim your creative passions and start writing! Here are some ways to connect with creativity and generate more of it:

Try This

1. Object Writing

As described by Pat Pattison in his book *Writing Better Lyrics,* Object Writing is a technique for developing sensory exploration and diving deeper faster. Object writing requires you to select any real object and set a timer for 10 minutes. Then write about the object freely – no need for complete sentences, proper grammar, correct spelling or rhyme. Tap into all 5 senses as well as the Kinesthetic (sense of relation to the world around you – drunk, moving, blurred vision) and Organic (heartbeat, pulse, breathing).

Try to be as vivid and imaginative as possible, using each of the senses. At the end of 10 minutes, stop writing. The idea is that, when done on a daily basis, the ability to tap into imagination quickens and our writing gets better, in the same way practicing scales develops instrumental technique. I get my students to do this every day for several weeks, and I can attest to the way it develops a stronger sense of figurative language and emotional connection (and many of these exercises have made their way into actual songs).

2. Artist's Dates

This is an idea borrowed from Julia Cameron. Head out on a solo excursion to a restaurant, café, park, or on whatever outing sounds like fun. The point is to do something that inspires playing, questioning, noticing, and replenishes your creative reservoir. Be protective of this time and resist the urge to involve others. Eavesdrop, cavort, be a voyeur and re-charge.

3. Artist's Routine

One of the best ways to build the creative muscle is to develop a routine. Work out every day at the same time and commit to specific goals. Do your Object Writing, write a verse, create a song plan, try a new song structure, use some new chords. Focused practice always leads to great results, and this holds true for creativity. I find it helps to plan the night before what you intend to work on the next day because it allows your subconscious time to work on the matter, and it creates expectation that your Muse will appear. By showing up regularly with intention, you learn to harness your creativity and channel it.

4. Raise Your Level of Curiosity

Writer and mythologist Joseph Campbell said to follow your bliss. I've always loved this maxim for both its simplicity and its soulfulness, and I hope this is at least part of what is driving you to want to express yourself. However, I understand author Elizabeth Gilbert when she warns that following your bliss might put too much pressure on yourself. She advocates following your curiosity instead. Thus, the mere act of showing up can be celebrated, mistakes freely made and creativity built into the fabric of everyday life.

Creativity needs curiosity, so cultivate yours. Investigate things you know nothing about and go places you've never been. Mess around with a second language; listen to interesting podcasts or video presentations. Go to a lecture or a concert you might not otherwise be drawn to. Look for the stories around you, and if there aren't any – imagine them by studying strangers and inventing stories about them based on the details of what you see or hear, or try to look at the world through another's eyes. Be interested and pay attention. Raising your level of curiosity will make your music more interesting, and it will make you more interesting, too.

5. Be Patient and Kind to Yourself

Patience is the quickest way to accomplish anything. So pluck up your courage and try stuff! As you do, allow yourself to be as bad as you have to be. There are no wrong answers here, only better ones. In almost any field of endeavour, no one ever became great without being non-great first. Writer Malcolm Gladwell's theory of 10,000 hours comes to mind as a typical breakpoint after which people begin to master their craft. And even then, any pro songwriter will tell you they come up with lots of flushable ideas along with the compelling ones.

Negative feelings probably are the result of comparing yourself to others. We should only ever compare ourselves to ourselves, as it is the one measure that really matters. There will always be somebody better and always somebody whom you are better than, so this scale is irrelevant. The true goal, in my opinion, is to follow Thelonius Monk's adage and try to be "the one most like himself."

Structure

Our brains are wired to continually scan for understanding. Human beings are bombarded with sensory information, well beyond our capacity to process all of it. In order to function without being overwhelmed, we learn from a young age to filter out what's unimportant and allow into our consciousness only what we think matters. Since this might change at any given moment, we're always assessing our environment and the events unfolding before us, checking for comprehension and framing what happens in a way that makes sense. As listeners, we love the certainty a healthy dose of repetition provides in music (as it confirms our understanding); and in contrast, we get frustrated when a lyric doesn't "add up." If listeners struggle to make sense of our song, they'll soon lose interest. Often, it's the way the pieces of a song are put together, more than the content itself, that is to blame.

Song form can function like well-designed architecture that allows easy access to various levels and spaces with facility and beauty, or like a poorly crafted building that's uninviting, confusing to navigate, and a place you never want to go back to. Bad structure creates barriers while effective structure welcomes you in.

Another way to think of structure is as a delivery system for your song. When the content of your song is well packaged and clearly marked, the likelihood your song will arrive safely at its intended destination is greatly enhanced.

Compared to the heady excitement of creating new ideas for a song, labouring over structure can seem like a buzzkill to a novice writer. So why do the best songwriters think it's so important?

To quote Québécoise songwriter Danièle Faubert:

"Structure forms the skeleton of your song. It is not a mould to artificially pour your lyrics into. It's a frame you build to showcase your lyrics or music in the best possible way. Form isn't the crux—it's the lyrics and music that bring originality and tone. However, (through form) you can explore different arrangement possibilities and seek the best possible interpretation for your song."
From Écrire une chanson, Vol. 2 (translation mine)

Let's look at the building blocks of Song Form.

Song Form – Basic Ingredients

Intro(duction)

Most songs begin with some kind of Intro. This is often a musical idea that sets the song up. It can build, layering in new instruments as it goes, set a groove or be the main hook (Satisfaction, Back In Black). A good Intro can set a mood, draw the listener in and build anticipation for the vocal.

Verse

Most songs offer a Verse as the first sung material (although a current trend starts with the chorus). This is where the lyrics establish Who, Where, When and possibly Why and What. In the Verses, stories are told, characters are developed, situations are explained and the lyric moves forward.

Pre-Chorus

Most current songs flow from Verse to Chorus, but many songs also incorporate a Pre-Chorus as a device to bridge Verse and Chorus and set up the Chorus in a stronger way. Many songwriters refer to this is as "the Lift" because it lifts the song into the Chorus. It does this in a number of ways.

Musically, the Pre-Chorus often enters new territory from both a melodic and/or a harmonic standpoint. New chords may appear, or a new riff, and the singer will most often sing notes that are a little higher than in the Verse (thereby helping "lift" the song and driving up the energy).

The Pre-Chorus is also a place to create some tension, and perhaps destabilize the music. This may involve adding or dropping a bar or a beat; repeating and building on a single chord to create anticipation; or generally building a sense of tension and instability so that when the Chorus arrives, there's a strong sense of arrival on solid ground.

Lyrically, this can also be a place for change. Lyric cadence may get faster or slower, take on a new rhyme scheme, and perhaps heighten anticipation by posing a question or creating a situation that the Chorus needs to address or respond to.

Pre-Choruses, appearing 2-3 times in most songs, are often similar to one another, but the lyrics are rarely repeated intact. If they were, the listener would be getting too much repetition because the Chorus is repeated as well, and the only lyrical change would be occurring in the Verses. Pre-Choruses tend to be a hybrid straddling the line between direct repetition and total variation by resembling one another, but not being identical.

Chorus

In general, the Chorus is the most memorable part of the song – what you walk away singing. Here is where the key message usually gets delivered, where the answer is found to the question "what's this song about?" and where the title is most often sung. This section normally gets repeated 2-5 times.

Refrain

The term Refrain is often substituted for Chorus, but they are not the same thing. Whereas a Chorus is a fully developed section, often similar in length to the Verse, the Refrain usually consists of only a few lines (or maybe just one). Refrains commonly occur in older song forms that don't feature Choruses, and frequently express the title of the song at the conclusion of a Verse (A Section), and possibly the Bridge or "Middle 8" (B Section). Famous songs that feature Refrains include Yesterday (I believe in yesterday), Don't Get Around Much Anymore, and The Sound of Silence.

In the past, some people referred to the Refrain as the most catchy recurring section of a Chorus, but this is usually called a Hook nowadays, and Hooks can occur anywhere in the song.

Re-Intro

A re-statement of the Intro idea often happens after the first Chorus (and possibly again later), and this is called, well, a Re-Intro. The length of the Re-Intro is frequently pared down from its original length because: a) we've heard it before, and it can be boring to overstate it, and b) the vocal has been established, and the role of the Re-Intro shifts from setting up the vocal to providing some relief from it. In practical terms, this means that if the Intro pattern is performed twice, the Re-Intro usually happens only once.

Bridge

The role of the Bridge is to offer contrast. Not all songs have them, but the ones that incorporate a Bridge usually do so to maintain the listener's interest, create musical dynamics or offer a lyrical aspect that has not been explored elsewhere.

Musically

Bridges are most often found after the second Chorus, about ⅔ of the way through the song (those familiar with the principle of the Golden Mean will recognize this), and can shake things up in several ways:

- Incorporate harmony (chords) not featured elsewhere.
- Change the rhythm of the accompaniment (i.e. if chords change every 2 bars, change them every bar, or every 4 bars).
- Change the groove (i.e. double-time, half-time, or find a new

hook), or alter the overall feel by either increasing intensity, or by diminishing it (a current trend).

- Change the rhythm of the melody.
- Alter the melodic contour. This is often where the highest note of the song can be found and the most passion delivered. When pitch rises, intensity builds (energy increases).

LYRICALLY

- State a message or introduce an idea not broached elsewhere.
- Reveal a new point of view, or a lyrical "twist" that adds a different colour to the meaning or spirit of the final chorus.
- Change the rhyme scheme and/or rhythm of the lyrics.

Hit songwriter Steve Seskin uses the following process to determine whether a song needs a Bridge from a lyrical point of view:

- If there's nothing left to say, don't write a Bridge (maybe go to a Solo).
- If there's lots left to say, write another Verse.
- If there's only a little left to say, write a Bridge.

Solos (or Musical Interludes)

Solos usually appear before a Bridge, after a Bridge, or instead of one. The reason to have a Solo in a song is to change voices so:

- The listener gets a break from the singer (no matter how great the singer is, we still usually want some "relief" from the musical monologue, just like in conversation).

- The music can offer a supporting emotional and artistic contribution that can elevate the song.
- Anticipation for the singer's return is established.

An important consideration for a solo section is what harmonic pattern to use. The goal is to maintain a structure that is interesting and not overly repetitive.

- If the Solo is going to be followed by a Verse, consider soloing over the Bridge pattern, the Chorus pattern or creating a new chord progression.
- If the Solo is to be followed by a Chorus (or a Pre-Chorus), consider soloing over the Verse pattern, Bridge pattern or Pre-Chorus pattern, if there is one.

Tag

The Tag is a short section that gets repeated at the end of a song. It is often the Refrain, or the last few lines of the last Chorus.

Outro

The Outro usually refers to the Intro (or Re-Intro) when it gets placed at the end of a song. It often features more development (maybe some improvised soloing or singing), but is based on the main idea of the Intro.

Rideout/Vamp

The defining feature of a Rideout or a Vamp at the end of a song is that it is constructed of new musical material and repeats. A famous example is Hey Jude.

Song Form - Structures

The above is a fairly exhaustive list of the ingredients you'll find in the forms of most songs. Let's look at how they go together.

Verse/Chorus Form

If you listen to practically any style of music today, you will notice most songs use forms that feature the alternation of Verses and Choruses. This combination works well because it satisfies the listener's need for repetition (Chorus), and variation (Verse). To keep things interesting, the songwriter might also include other such elements as Intro, Re-Intro, Bridge, Solo and Outro. Here are a few examples of some common Verse/Chorus forms:

Example 1	Example 2	Example 3	Example 4
Intro	Intro	Chorus	Intro
Verse	Verse	Verse	Verse
Chorus	Verse	Chorus	Pre-Chorus
Re-Intro	Chorus	Verse	Chorus
Verse	Verse	Bridge	Re-Intro
Chorus	Chorus	Solo	Verse
Bridge	Bridge	Chorus	Pre-Chorus
Solo	Chorus	Vamp	Chorus
Chorus	Chorus		Solo
Outro			Pre-Chorus
			Chorus
			Tag

Song structures will vary depending on what the song itself is calling for artistically, and on such considerations as length (is it too long?

Too short?), and the sense of flow. This last variable, flow, is what I otherwise refer to as "energy management." To this end, the way a song is structured can play a key role in how the energy of the song is perceived.

People tune out if the Intro bogs down, the Chorus takes too long to get to, the Solo comes too soon, if the Verses or Re-Intro are too long and if things become too predictable or boring. Sometimes songs need built-in "breathing room" between sections, or editing to remove unnecessary measures. The arrangement and production of the song also play a vital role here, but if the structure of the song works, the arrangement will work that much better.

New Developments

It's interesting to note that since the onset of the digital age, more and more songs begin with Choruses. The reason often cited for this is people now seek out new music online instead of on the radio. So musicians are offering instant gratification for the listener by placing the Chorus first. This can create problems for song structure, though, because it might mean the Chorus appears too frequently, and risks boring the listener by the 3rd or 4th iteration. In response, a heightened focus has been placed on production to keep the listener's attention, and new twists like repeating the Bridge and adding rap sections are being used to avoid overexposing the Chorus.

There has been a growing trend in recent years toward eliminating the Bridge from songs (Sorry by Adele, Love Yourself by Justin Bieber, Can't Feel My Face by The Weeknd). Writers Andy Smarick and

Bernard Lee Schwartz argue the Bridge has been headed for collapse for a long time, citing a number of older songs (Unchained Melody, Can't Help Falling In Love, Let My Love Open the Door) whose Bridges served to derail and undermine what are otherwise great songs. Whether or not you agree with Smarick and Lee about these cases, their point is that, when Bridges are bad, they're really bad, and can often lead to disaster. To quote Smarick and Schwartz, "what's so worrisome about today's songwriters is that they seem to have recognized the bridge challenge, turned tail and run." As alternatives, artists are choosing other devices like solos, breaking the music down (a Breakdown involves stripping away parts of the accompaniment like drums and bass, or lessening the intensity of the performance), modulating to a higher key for the final chorus or adding a new voice (i.e. a rapper or a singer).

Another trend is the Breakdown Bridge. In the past, most Bridges were a rallying point, the climax of the song and the place with the highest intensity. Many artists are now going in the other direction, lowering the intensity level and then building back up after the Bridge. This device can work well, but the challenge is to not kill the vibe of the song and lose the listener's interest.

Classic Forms

It may be hard to believe, but before the 1960s, few songs had Choruses like we see today. Some believe the advent of the Verse/Chorus song came with the introduction of FM radio in the '70s, where stations, unbound by the hit formats of AM radio, felt free to play longer and generally more adventurous songs in a better-sounding audio format.

Before then, the Work song, Folk songs, songs from Musicals and songs being created in New York's Tin Pan Alley, and later the Brill Building, were simpler, and made more use of the Refrain. Such older structures can be described best in terms of how sections (e.g. A Section, B Section, etc.) are ordered. Below are some common older forms (which all still work very well).

AAA: This basic structure is still the best choice for story-telling, character development, and moving a story through changing time frames. This form is usually more lyric-focused than melody-focused. With such a simple form, the onus is on the songwriter to create exceptional lyrics and a catchy Refrain.

Examples: Amazing Grace, Blowin' In The Wind (three-line refrain), Bridge Over Troubled Water, I Walk The Line, By The Time I Get To Phoenix.

AABA: This form introduces a contrasting section, and was a favourite of Tin Pan Alley and Musical Theatre writers. Often the lyrics flow in an uninterrupted (linear) expression of one's feelings or a specific situation, and it practically demands a single time frame, a consistent viewpoint and an unchanging setting.

Musically, it should be noted that each A Section may end differently than the one before it. The first A Section often concludes in an Open Ending (avoiding the root of the key) and a Turn-around (a musical device that draws the ear forward in a sense of continuity, and in this case, setting up another statement of the A Section). The Second

A Section can end with either a Closed or Open Ending and has no Turn-around as it heads into the new material of the B Section. The final A Section usually ends with Closed Ending (which sounds final), and frequently features a Tag of the Refrain.

Examples: Take The A-Train, Misty, Satin Doll, I Got Rhythm, Blue Moon, Over The Rainbow, Crazy.

ABAB: At first glance, this looks identical to a Verse/Chorus structure. Unlike the Verse/Chorus format, however, it makes one big section out of 2 distinct smaller sections, and creates a more cohesive unit out of A and B together. A famous example is Fly Me To The Moon (a.k.a. In Other Words).

Note that the final B Section may end differently from the preceding ones because the other B Sections need to return to the A section, while the final B Section usually concludes the song.

ABAC is a rarer form that involves following each iteration of the main idea (A Section) with brand new material. Moon River is a good example.

Another song form, the Art Song, puts poetry to music, can be strophic (using repetition) or through-composed (with little or no repetition). Such music is generally found in the classical sphere, with Schubert, Schumann, Brahms, Mahler, Richard Strauss, Wagner, Schoenberg, Ives, Vaughan Williams and Britten being famous practitioners.

An alternate form that became popular with composers is the Song Cycle. This involves organizing songs into groupings of common themes, ideas, emotions or events, which, when performed in sequence create a unified work. Beethoven, Ravel, Debussy and most of the composers listed above wrote Song Cycles, but this convention has also carried over to recent times, in works by such artists as the Beatles (Sgt. Pepper, Abbey Road), Stevie Wonder (Songs in the Key of Life) and Billy Joel (The Stranger).

Finally, the form that has had the biggest influence on Popular Music is undoubtedly the Blues form. This simple structure has its origins in African American slave songs, and has provided the underpinning for Jazz, Rock, Folk, Country and all the other forms that grew out of them. As John Lennon famously said: "The blues is a chair, not a design for a chair or a better chair ... it is the first chair. It is a chair for sitting on, not for looking at. You sit on that music."

In its most basic state, the Blues form uses a repetitive 12 bar chord progression and features one or two antecedent phrases followed by a consequent phrase.

Examples: Baby Please Don't Go (Muddy Waters), Crossroads Blues (Robert Johnson), Further On Up The Road (Eric Clapton).
The Blues is very much alive today in its traditional forms, and its presence is also being felt in modern Pop, R&B, Jazz, Folk and many other crossover styles. It remains an important and relevant style for all songwriters to know how to use.

Recording vs. Live

When it comes to selecting a form, different audiences will dictate different choices. For instance, in a live environment, artists will often extend sections, get the crowd to sing along, play around with dynamics, and generally mould the form into a structure that maximizes the live experience. This more open approach can be perfect for a live audience, but often misses the mark when it comes to recorded music.

One consideration is that a live crowd has already taken a supportive action by simply showing up. This means the audience is predisposed to embrace your music in anticipation of a positive experience. With recorded music, however, the listener is often more discerning (especially such industry gatekeepers as publishers, managers, labels, producers, etc.), and the song will be competing with other songs, and other distractions, for the attention of the listener. In this environment, songwriters need to maximize their chances of cutting through the noise, and a well-constructed song stands a much better chance of being heard.

Try This

1. Analyze the song structures of classic songs across generational lines and in a wide variety of styles. What patterns do you notice? What does the form do to help the song? Consider what would have happened if other choices had been made. Analyze how it is that you can distinguish one section from the next, and pay attention to the general shapes the melody takes, how energy is managed, and any other distinguishing features of harmony and rhythm.

2. *Identify the structures of the following songs*: The Times They Are A-Changin' (Bob Dylan), Somewhere Over the Rainbow (from The Wizard of Oz), Yesterday (Beatles), Sunny Came Home (Shawn Colvin) and Kings (Steely Dan). Answers are below.

3. *Select a structure and write a lyric, a melody or an entire song based on it.* Incorporate the same rhyming patterns, the same order of the various sections, and use repetition and variation in places the original did.

Answers:

The Times They Are A-Changin' (Bob Dylan):
Intro, A, Re-Intro, A, A, A, Outro

Somewhere Over the Rainbow (Harold Arlen & E.Y. Harburg):
A, A, B, A, C (short ending section)

Yesterday (John Lennon & Paul McCartney):
Intro A A B A B A Tag

Sunny Came Home (Shawn Colvin & John Leventhal):
Intro A, B, Re-Intro, A, B, C (breakdown Bridge), B,
B'(different lyrics, extended), Outro

Kings (Walter Becker & Donald Fagen):
Intro, V, Pre-Ch, Ch, V2, Pre-Ch2, Ch2, Instr. Bridge, Solo, Pre3, Ch3, Tag,
Bridge as Vamp

Music Theory

For some, music theory is a fascinating subject that explores the sonic metrics of the cosmos to reveal its mystical properties. For others, it's a necessary evil. Either way, the more you know, the more able you will be to find solutions to problems as they arise. When you understand how music gets put together, you can harness the power to make your music go where you want, while enjoying the freedom to follow it where it wants to take you.

The scope of this book does not include a detailed discussion of music theory. This is because post-secondary music students and professionals working with the book already have a strong theory foundation, and readers with a less formal background would be best advised to learn about theory as a parallel but separate endeavour. To this end, I did write a book, *Bob's Book of Music Theory*, where readers can start from zero, or fill in missing pieces, and arm themselves with necessary information. I won't go any further plugging the book, other than to say it is available on Amazon (www.createspace.com/3753294). Of course, many other books are also available that will help you learn about the mechanics of music.

Having said this, most aspiring songwriters have some understanding of scales and chords, and I hope that what follows will be of benefit to all (and hopefully spur some readers to dive in deeper with theory and harmony).

The Point Is ...

- Reading and writing the language of music are not requirements for a songwriter. But fluency is an important resource. Knowing how music works enables you to analyze situations accurately when problems arise, and gives you the vision to see a wider field of possibilities.
- Reading music is a skill. It's a great asset for communicating and cataloguing ideas, and if you want to make a living as a musician for hire, it's practically essential. However, it is not a requirement for being a songwriter. Don't confuse musical literacy with musical comprehension.
- Understanding music offers access to all forms of music as a listener and allows you to listen critically. This will help your songwriting.

Real-life Theory Considerations for the Songwriter ...

Chord Choices

At some point, most songwriters fall into the rut of repeating the same chords within a song or from one song to another, and this can make the music feel stagnant and predictable. But there is always another option to the chord you are playing.

Every melody note has a minimum of three chord choices. This is because basic chords are formed in triads, and any given note can function as one of the three notes in a triad. For instance, the note C is the first note of C Major triad, the second note in an Ab Major triad, and the third note in an F Major triad, so any one of these chords is an option for harmonizing the note C.

As we move into four-note, five-note, six-note and even larger chords, the possibilities for harmonizing a melody increase exponentially. Having access to a wider selection of chords gives you the tools to choose the most desirable chord for your melody at any given time, and this, in turn, gives you the ability to make your song as harmonically simple or complex as you feel it should be. In concrete terms, it gives songwriters access to a larger sonic canvas, and allows us to add dashes of colour to even the most straightforward styles of music.

Any melody can be harmonized in myriad ways. How you do this may depend on style, emotional content of the lyrics and level of complexity desired. For example, Renée Fleming's symphonic arrangement of Over the Rainbow features rich five and six-note chords, pedal point and counter melodies. In contrast, versions of the same song by Israel "IZ" Kamakawiwo'ole and Eva Cassidy offer beautifully simple renderings with just one voice and a single chord instrument. Each version uses different chords to harmonize the same song, and the original version sung by Judy Garland uses yet another chord progression. Each one of these arrangements is suited to the specific singer and the occasion, and delivers a different feeling.

It's always good to have a second look at your chord progressions to see if there might be better choices, especially if:

- The same chord appears regularly (i.e. every four bars).
- The chorus features some or all of the verse chords.
- The bridge repeats previously heard chords.
- The music feels boring or predictable.

When you're looking for other possibilities, a good question to ask is: "What other chords will support the melody?" For instance, in the key of A Major, the note "A" can be found in the following diatonic chords: AMajor, F#minor and DMajor. Note that a relative Major or minor triad are only one note different.

If we extend our search to include diatonic 7th chords, we can now add AMaj7, Bm7, DMaj7, and F#m7.

If we extend our search even further, by borrowing from other keys or expanding our range of possibilities in more chromatic directions, we can find many more options. Some of the more useful ones include: FMaj7, F7, Gadd9, C6/9, Dm, Dm6, E7sus, B7, BbMaj7. With so many different ways to go, decisions can be based on a sense of personal inspiration and artistic sensibility.

For more on the relationship between melody and harmony (chords), as well as developing bass lines with chords, **please see Chapter 9, "Melody."**

Writing in Styles

Each form of music has stylistic markers that you can incorporate in your music. This is especially important if you need to work within an identifiable genre, as often happens when you are asked to write for a specific artist, film or other collaborative project.

Harmonic choices can have a direct impact on the music and the listener (who is likely unaware that certain sounds create distinct associations and reveal clear preferences), and help identify a style. For instance, much of Rock, Country and Folk music sticks to simple harmony that uses only a handful of diatonic chords. So if the task is to create a song for, say, a traditional story-telling folk singer, jazzy chords may not serve the music, and can present a barrier in this style. However, within the broader umbrella of Rock, Folk and Country, certain sub-genres do stray into more adventurous harmonic territory (for instance, all three styles borrow from modal music - from Led Zeppelin and Bill Monroe to Fairport Convention), and an awareness of the relevant stylistic markers can help you determine where these lines blur, and how.

Other defining features can be seen clearly through the lens of theory. Such contrapuntal music as madrigals and fugues feature interweaving parts that follow strict rules (i.e. no parallel fifths or octaves and no tritones), while free-form jazz decrees only that the players listen to one another (and this usually means being able to discern intervals and keys). Much medieval music is modal in nature; Flamenco music features the Spanish-Phrygian scale; Celtic music frequently uses Dorian and Mixolydian scales and pedal point/drones; Bluegrass, Asian and North American Indigenous music share Pentatonic scales; Blues, Pop, Country and Rock often quote the Blues scale; Metal is based in minor scales that also feature tritons and chromaticism (with few chords); and Jazz uses a wide variety of diatonic, modal and altered scales. To write in a particular style, it helps to be able to pick out what is going on harmonically (i.e. use of scales and chords) and stylistically (i.e. use of ornaments, affectations, instrumental and vocal techniques), and build these elements into your music.

It's also good to have a grasp of what is being done rhythmically. The majority of music the world over is in $^4/_4$ time, but certain styles predominantly feature other time signatures: $^6/_8$ (Jigs, Marches), $^{12}/_8$ (Blues), $^2/_4$ (Country, Reels, Horas, Polkas), $^3/_4$ (Country, Waltz, Jazz), $^5/_4$ (Jazz and Spy Movie Themes). Classical music uses every conceivable time signature. Rock music frequently features straight eighth notes, while Swing turns eighth notes into a form of triplets. Jazz is often played behind the beat, while Metal and Disco are "on top," and Afro-Cuban, Afro-Brazilian and "Latin" music feature a variety of key rhythms (claves) that are the backbone of the music. The deeper you delve into any genre, the more you will find style-specific uses of beat, groove and rhythm.

What you do with time, and the key (with its related harmonies) you choose to write in, set the tempo and tone of your musical landscape. Different feels and keys will create different moods that lyrics will want to match, and will also give clear indications of genre. One of the best ways to get to know a style is to transcribe music to see what the musicians are doing. What kind of time signatures, rhythms and tempos do they use? What is the harmony doing – is there a repeating chord progression, bass line or ostinato; is there counterpoint or pedalpoint; are chords simple or complex?

Since songwriters are often expected to be their own producers, a final consideration involves creating an arrangement that enhances the style you want to convey. Choice of instruments, sounds, attitude, ambience and approach all figure into the arrangement, and put finishing touches on the song's final presentation.

Identifying Problems and Finding Solutions

When things don't sound right, an analytical approach will help you identify the problem and find a solution. This is very useful when chords and melody are clashing, vocal harmonies sound off, or if timing is uncertain. It can help you figure out why a melody is static or why a chorus isn't hitting like it should. It's also very helpful in live settings when something doesn't sound right, and you can identify the problem and adjust on the fly.

This may require examining what chords are being played and pin-pointing non-chord tones (notes that don't belong in the chord). Such notes can clash significantly, especially when accented, and too many of them can make the melody sound very wrong. Solutions might involve changing melody notes or changing the chords.

Sometimes chords have wrong notes that don't belong in the song's key. A quick analysis of the melody can determine the underlying key of the song (based on the scale used by the melody), and stray notes in chords and bass lines quickly ferreted out.

Problems with a melody's contour and rhythm can also be spotlighted if you examine how use of range and rhythm is affecting the energy of the song. Sometimes a chorus doesn't have much impact because the melody descends when it should rise, or if the cadence of the melody is static. An analytical approach can help determine if certain notes or chords are being overused, if a rhythm appears too often or if a range is too limited **(please see Chapter 9, Melody, for more)**.

Finally, there might be clashes or disagreements in rhythm and feel between musicians that can be ironed out by analyzing where players are interpreting a feel differently, misunderstanding how certain rhythms get played, or even misinterpreting time signatures or miscounting.

Finding Cool Stuff

Finally, a good grasp of theory will allow you to more easily and consistently craft interesting bass lines, create hooks that work with a melody or a groove, invent compelling melodies, and create tension and release in your writing. With a fuller tool kit, you'll be able to see more possibilities for your music at the outset, and add interesting touches that provide polish and originality.

Lyrics – Theory and Perspective

If you're like me, a great deal of your favourite music is instrumental. So, if music doesn't require singing or lyrics to succeed, why have them?

Part of the answer can be found in a listener's affinity for the voice. Speech is an innate part of human expression, and listeners, equipped with their own voices, can generally relate more strongly to a sung melody than an instrumental one. Non-musicians more easily perceive inflection and nuance and, in the end, people pick up on a singer's attitude and energy more readily than an instrumentalist's.

And of course, the other part of the equation is what happens when great music is combined with great lyrics. What emerges is a third entity that has tremendous power and potential.

Lyrics vs. Poetry

Many people equate good lyric-writing with good poetry. In truth, most lyrics, when taken without music, will not yield even passable poetry. And the reason is simple: lyrics are not poetry.

By definition, songs contain both music and lyrics. Lyrics are not intended to stand independent of the music – they belong to the larger work, and are meant to be sung. Lyrics have to conform to the rhythmic demands of the melody, adhere to a rhyme scheme that is supported or suggested by the music, and importantly, have to sound musical. The stresses of the words themselves must make sense when phrased by the singer to be understood. As all songwriters find out, the most perfect word can sound terrible when sung.

Poetry, by contrast, has no constraints of any kind. The words are intended to be read silently or aloud with no temporal restrictions, and they form the entirety of the work. Once upon a time, there were conventions of meter and rhyme, but those days are gone and poets are free to take as long as necessary to say whatever they want.

If poetry is a monologue, lyrics are sound bites, and they're required to do more work in less time. Most songs contain only 100-200 non-repeating words, so the lyricist, working with few tools (the number of words) and a demanding partner (the music), must make the most out of each line, and this requires the ability to focus on function as well as artistry, and to edit accordingly. As a result, lyrics often sound more simple than poetry. But the ability to craft a succinct lyric can be painstaking and time-consuming. This quote attributed to author Mark Twain is emblematic of the nature of lyric writing:

"I didn't have time to write a short letter, so I wrote you a long one instead."

In an art form that uses time as its canvas, lyrics often need to be pared down in order to stand out against the competing demands of sound and rhythm, and be understood as the song goes by. As well, it often has more impact to use vocabulary that is conversational, enabling the listener to relate to the singer through direct and accessible language.

This is not to say that lyrics cannot be poetic. Songwriters make frequent use of figurative language (metaphor, hyperbole, personification, symbolism, simile, etc.) to tell their stories, paint their pictures and convey their messages. It is just within a more restrictive framework than most other forms of writing.

Practise

Musicians know the importance of practising their instrument. Intention, focus and repetition are key elements in acquiring most skills, and lyric writing is no different.

We usually think of practise as an action. However, practise also requires paying attention. When you listen actively or study the work of great lyricists, you begin to notice the choices they make, understand how they approach their art, and get deeper inside the craft. If you analyze the lyrics to some of your favourite artists' best songs, what do you notice? Do they hit you on an emotional level? Why or why not? Can you easily tell what the song is about? Do the lyrics always add up?

One of my favourite songwriters is Paul Simon. Besides being a great melodist, he has the ability to craft unforgettably vivid lines. However, at the end of many of his songs, I find myself wondering what the song meant, what conclusions to draw: what was the point of the song? I feel the same way about some of the other greats of his generation like the Beatles and Leonard Cohen. All are masters of the phrase, but not always the complete song (as a case in point, the debate over the meaning of Cohen's Hallelujah has been raging for decades).

Still, they all had great careers, right? Absolutely. And this is seen by some as a testament to the power of music to triumph over lyrics. But remember that each era is different, and it was stylistically acceptable to write that way in the '60s and '70s (John Lennon made a career out of writing stream of consciousness lyrics). Most up-and-coming songwriters are judged by a new set of standards, and having lyrics make sense is a skill you're going to need in today's marketplace.

Try This

1. *Have a look at Joni Mitchell's work and examine how she was so adept at making her lyrics poetic and captivating, yet also coming to conclusions and telling stories* (her songs Raised on Robbery, River and Woodstock are good starting points). Or study the album *Jagged Little Pill* by Alanis Morrisette to learn why her lyrics galvanized a generation of young women. Try a few classics like: What a Wonderful World (Thiele/Weiss), I Will Survive (Freddie Perren), She's In Love With The Boy (Jon Ims), Up On The Roof (Goffin and King), The Heart of the Matter (Don Henley), I'll Never Fall In Love Again (Bacharach/David), Dear Mama (2Pac), Firework (Katy Perry) – the list goes on. What is it about these songs that connected with so many people?

2. *If you're stuck in line somewhere, killing time or out on an artist's date, take a good look at strangers* (but don't be creepy!). I know a number of people who take people-watching to the next level. What personality traits can you deduce from their physical characteristics? Imagine their back story, give them names, construct relationships and fabricate a conflict, romance or other situation for the people you are observing, or with an imaginary person if the stranger is solo. What is the mood or emotion conveyed? What will happen next? This exercise will develop your skills of observation, dial you into the potential for human drama and possibly lead to a story worth telling.

A variation on this is to read an article or watch a (news) story about an event, and imagine the scenario from the point of view of a person who didn't figure prominently in the story, but was involved. What insights would they have? How does this situation affect the life of that person?

3. Now put your observational skills into practice by setting one of the above stories or situations to lyrics. It might help to borrow a rhyme scheme and a structure from a song you know. How should it be told? Who will do the talking? What specifics should make their way into the song? We will go into more detail about these questions later, but for now, practise seeing the stories around you – real or imaginary – and start writing them down.

Managing the Listener's Imagination

Before we get into the nuts and bolts of lyric writing, it would be good to have some discussion about listeners and the nature of their imagination so that you use your writer's tools to the fullest advantage.

Chris Blake, a contributor to John Braheny's *The Craft and Business of Songwriting*, describes the imagination as wild, in a constant state of readiness, and considers it a determining factor in whether a listener will be interested in your song. Imagination, always on standby, has no choice but to act, and only needs a trigger to set it off (be it an internal thought or external stimulus). Any new trigger will distract it and send it spiralling off in new directions. As the songwriter, you want to control the trigger at all times.

It's interesting to note that, while songwriters often write about such abstract universal themes as love, sadness, jealousy, etc., the imagination can't relate to these concepts without specific and detailed language. The imagination wants to know Who, What, When, How and Why. It wants shiny details to attract its attention and a compelling set of events to keep it. And so it is that the imagination requires the writer to show and not tell.

Picture two young women who have been friends since high school, but who haven't seen each other for a year. They get together for lunch, and one announces: "So, guess what? I'm in love." Would the conversation end there? Of course not! The friend would demand details. It's another way of saying, "Show me what you mean." How did you meet, how long have you known each other, what is the person like, looks, name, occupation, hometown, etc. – these specifics create a picture, and set a tone for the emotion behind the circumstances.

To the imagination, "I love you" barely registers. "I love you, hands full" (Menard/Walsh) adds a provocative twist. Compare "you're lying" to "you can't hide your lyin' eyes" (Henley/Frey). Or how about "a nice car" vs. "Little Red Corvette" (Prince); "Pink Cadillac" (Springsteen) or "Little Deuce Coupe" (Wilson/Christian).

Notice how the above examples are simple images that are singular in focus. They strike the imagination with impact and ease. When images become too complicated or diverse, it feels like work to the imagination to sort them out, and listeners can get bogged down just trying to figure out what they're hearing.

If you want to harness the imagination, feed it specifics, and keep things simple ("simple" doesn't mean un-poetic or dumbed-down). And don't stop – the imagination will get bored and abandon you. If you deliver the particulars, it will tune in. Rely on generalities, it tunes out. And keep things moving.

Action creates experience. The mind's eye loves detail, but it might love action more. Consider any personal experience: something had to happen to make it an event. This is because life doesn't unfold in the abstract. It's a moment-to-moment experiential reality. If you want to heighten a listener's experience, combine specifics with action. In doing so, you can reveal the essence of a concept or an abstraction in a way the imagination can't resist.

For instance, what if Patrick Henry (U.S Founding Father) had said: "Being executed is preferable to existing without freedom"? I doubt he would have inspired the American people like he did when he said "Give me liberty or give me death." Notice how Henry used action (give me), avoided the abstract (being executed, existing without freedom) by using simple, singular and powerful words (liberty, death), and kept it short (memorable) and clear (easy for the imagination to rally behind).

Let's take a few ideas and mess with them. These are from student drafts:

The things you do make me want to know you
The way you look makes me want you bad

And here is the same idea, re-worked with specifics, simple language and action:

Electric shock when you brushed my shoulder
My knees gave in when you smiled at me

Another idea:

Glad you're gone, I'm carrying on. I'm so happy to be free again

Becomes more interesting:

Just me to please, one set of keys, and no one to say "where ya going"

One more:

It's hard sometimes when you can't find the words
To say what you want, and make your message heard

Tweaked:

Thoughts run aground like a stranded boat
Words get stuck in the back of my throat

Consider how all these songs use specific, simple, and action-based language: Fly Me To the Moon, Hit Me With Your Best Shot, While My Guitar Gently Weeps, Don't Take Your Guns to Town, London Calling, You Don't Learn That in School, Satan Gave Me A Taco, The Revolution Will Not Be Televised, Should I Stay Or Should I Go, Un-Break My Heart, Help, Cry Me a River, The First Time Ever I Saw Your Face, I Feel Lucky, Let's Give Them Something to Talk About, I've Got You Under My Skin, Started From the Bottom, Stop in the Name of Love. You may have noticed that most of these titles use the first person pronoun (I, me, my), explicitly or implicitly. The first person forms a stronger, more immediate connection with the listener.

Blake makes the point that the imagination can act only on what it knows. In other words, the sum of the listener's life experiences, both real and imaginary, are what form the reservoir of consciousness from which the songwriter can draw. If you're singing a song about a set of experiences that are outside the listener's background or personal framework, the imagination can't connect. For this reason, it's important to know your audience. People won't be able to relate if you write over their heads, and worse, you will sound pretentious or arrogant.

The tools used to engage the imagination – specifics, simplicity and action – are the tools to convey a more abstract or conceptual idea. Yet both aspects of writing will be found in songs. Songwriter Andrea Volpe, in her book *Popular Lyric Writing*, distinguishes between lyrics that describe what is going on around the main character "external details" (specifics), and those that describe what is going on in the heart or mind of the main character "internal details" (abstract). Both are necessary, but it's the external details that will illuminate the internal ones.

Try This

1. Select a theme like love, sorrow, romance, friendship or betrayal, and create a title or a first line that uses specifics and simple language. Try to make it come alive with vivid and clear images that spark the imagination.

2. Now see what happens if you alter your title or line by adding an action word.

Clarity

If the point of art is to communicate, then clarity is an important consideration. As discussed, the imagination gets annoyed when the music is hard to follow, boring or "doesn't add up." When it comes to lyrics, I would go further. I believe it can be lazy and cynical of the songwriter to write vaguely and avoid or obscure meaning by creating lyrics that are hard to understand and can be taken several ways. This usually means the writer hasn't spent enough time sorting out what they want to say (or doesn't know), or hasn't been brave enough to say what they actually mean. In any case, I feel it's often disrespectful to listeners who invest their time (and money) in good faith, only to have the artist hide behind ambiguity.

The most common argument against writing with clarity goes like this: "I want people to take away what they want from the lyrics, to interpret them whichever way they choose." While I agree that when it comes to most things, it's a good idea to not impose our views on others, this is not true of songwriting. People listen to find out what the artist has to say and it's a platform that exists for the purpose of expressing artistic individuality. This doesn't mean preaching, but it does mean asserting one's perspective in song. It may also mean learning something new in order to develop a point of view. Or it might require being vulnerable, and this can be scary. But it is also the main job of songwriters to be honest and tell their truth, so a little fear and uncertainty comes with the territory. In the end, it's simply much harder and more time-consuming to write with concision, and sometimes it takes courage to say what you really mean and put it on display. But this is what the art of songwriting asks of us.

If my argument in favour of clarity isn't convincing, I still recommend all songwriters acquire the skills to write clearly and intelligibly. In my mind it's like trying to play Jazz before you can play the Blues. If you can play the Blues, it'll provide a foundation for your Jazz playing and you'll get the benefit of the doubt when you play "outside." But if you can't play the Blues, the more sophisticated things you try to do in Jazz will risk sounding inauthentic and contrived.

Guard against writing " internalized" lyrics. This refers to text that the writer understands perfectly, but no one else can make sense of. This can happen to anyone at any level, but the more a person works at the craft, the more quickly they can catch themselves. Over time, the ability to look at lyrics objectively improves. Here are two strategies to start with: a) Have someone else look at the lyrics and tell you what they take away; b) Step away from the lyrics for awhile and come back later with fresh eyes and a new perspective. Pretend you're reading them for the first time. Does everything still add up?

Try This

Examine your lyrics as if you had never seen them before and knew nothing about the characters or situation. Does it all make sense? Does each line have enough setup or background to make it understandable? Are you assuming anything you shouldn't? Do events occur in the proper sequence? Do we always know who is talking and who is being talked about? Do the tenses move around? Are there inside jokes or expressions that most people won't know? Are you using metaphors that don't work? Are there any other barriers in the way of grasping the lyric's meaning and intent?

Symbols and Archetypes

Thus far the basis of our discussion has been the conscious mind. On a subconscious level, however, the imagination reacts less to words, and more to feelings, and these can be expressed strongly through symbols. We are all raised with images we internalize as members of the society and culture we grow up in, and each one has a particular meaning and can elicit a wide range of responses. Psychologist Carl Jung referred to this as the Collective Unconscious.

Think of the visceral reaction the swastika evokes even today, with young people several generations removed from World War II. (Ironically, for Hindus, Buddhists and others, it is a sacred symbol of well-being and good fortune.) Picture the cross, or a cross burning, or the Star of David, or the peace symbol and consider what feelings these images stir up. By extension, objects, places and things can also take on meaning. The Eiffel Tower signifies the City of Love, Wall Street conjures the image of greed and corporate America, and the

Berlin Wall represents isolationism, separation, communism vs. capitalism and, eventually, liberation and reconciliation. A single place setting implies loneliness or the loss of someone, rolled-up sleeves equals hard work, a skull represents danger or death.

When the Allman Brothers sang It Ain't My Cross to Bear, or the Beatles sang Lady Madonna (symbol of the Divine Feminine and Mother), they were moving past the intellect and heading directly for the subconscious, where we store the meaning of symbols and our emotional response to them.

Carl Jung also used the concept of archetype, the universal characters that reside in our collective unconscious, in his theory of the human psyche. Mythologist Joseph Campbell's work deconstructing archetypes in his book *The Hero with a Thousand Faces*, and his description of "the hero's journey" (a common transformational story pattern found the world over) influenced the creation of the movie Star Wars, and is valuable reading for anyone interested in storytelling. For our purposes, I simply want to illustrate that Jung's basic archetypes (and their shadow sides) can be found in song.

Here are 12 basic archetypes:

1. The Innocent
2. The Orphan/Everyman/Everywoman
3. The Hero
4. The Caregiver/Saint
5. The Explorer
6. The Rebel

7. The Lover
8. The Creator
9. The Jester
10. The Sage
11. The Magician
12. The Ruler

Songs that use archetypes include:
Redneck Woman (Gretchen Wilson, John Rich). The Everywoman.
Friends in Low Places (Blackwell/Lee). The Everyman.
Lady Madonna (Lennon/McCartney). The Caregiver/Saint.
Venus (Robbie Van Leeuwen). The Lover.
I Still Haven't Found What I'm Looking For (U2). The Explorer.
Ruby Tuesday. (Jagger/Richards). The Innocent.

Try This

1. ***Write a song that uses a symbol to illustrate its main theme or message.*** When used effectively, a symbol can replace many words. You might consider what subjects you would like to write about and how you could use a symbol to express your main idea.

2. ***Write a song based on an archetype.*** What events could unfold to reveal their nature and their significance? Is there another archetype who could be used as an antagonist to do this, or to create conflict?

Lyrics - Tools and Techniques

Now that we've had some discussion about how to approach lyric writing, it's time to roll up our sleeves.

The Title

As any good advertiser knows, a memorable catchphrase will go far in grabbing the public's attention and creating interest in what you're selling. If that interest can be converted into the potential buyer becoming emotionally involved with the product, they will use the rational reasons being promoted about its quality, price, etc., as justification for making the purchase. A similar thing occurs when it comes to trying to interest listeners in your music, and it becomes even more important if you want them to buy it.

As songwriters, our product is more than just a song – we are offering an experience. This means presenting a 3 or 4 minute journey that shifts listeners' emotions, whether through a fun groove, uplifting message, interesting story or a beautiful melody, and touches their heart and mind. In fact, the combination of music and lyrics is so powerful, it can connect with people beyond emotion and intellect. Music runs so deep for humans that we react viscerally as well – compelling us to sway, tap our toes, drum on our knees, clap our hands, dance and sing as a result of what we are hearing. This means your song has the potential to create a "whole-person" experience, drilling deep into feelings, thoughts and instincts.

As a starting point, develop a strong title that will invite the listener to take the journey.

"The public buys a song, not because it knows the song, but because it knows and likes the title idea."
Irving Berlin

"I write titles and work backwards from there."
Sting

Originality is the key to a great title, and for many songwriters, it's key to unlocking the song. Whether used as the main point of departure, or arrived at later, it is a good idea to make the title convey the main point or prevailing attitude of the song, and use it in an interesting, unexpected and imaginative way.

Some titles challenge the imagination: Jailhouse Rock, What If God Was One Of Us, I Kissed a Girl, A Hard Day's Night, The Tears of a Clown, Losing My Religion, One Bourbon, One Scotch, One Beer, Truly Madly Deeply, Ain't Nobody Here But Us Chickens.

Others express the focal point or main feeling of the song, almost like a promise to the listener of what will come: Happy, Let's Dance, Celebrate Good Times, Shake It Off, Missing You, I Want To Take You Higher, Feelin' Alright.

To find titles that will strike a common chord with the public, writers are always hunting for phrases they can either incorporate into a song

(Heard It Through the Grapevine, Once Bitten Twice Shy), make funny by changing its meaning (Act Naturally, My Wife Ran Off With My Best Friend And I Sure Do Miss Him) or alter (Friends In Low Places, Live and Let Die, No Shoes, No Shirt, No Problem).

Other techniques include:
Creating a visual: Tea for Two, You Can Leave Your Hat On, Sixteen Candles.

Playing with opposites (antonyms): I Got It Bad And That Ain't Good, Been Down So Long It Feels Like Up To Me, Full Moon and Empty Arms.

Posing a question: If I Told You You Had a Beautiful Body Would You Hold It Against Me, What's New Pussycat, What's Love Got To Do With It, Where Did Our Love Go.

Playing with the hypothetical: If I Had A Hammer, If I Fell, If I Were a Rich Man.

Using metaphor: You Ain't Nothing But a Hound Dog, Running On Empty, Bridge Over Troubled Waters.

Using simile: Like a Virgin, Walk Like an Egyptian, I'm Like a Bird.

Using devices that are easily remembered:

- Colours (Purple Rain, Green Tambourine, Blue Suede Shoes).
- Names (Angie, Hello Dolly, Sweet Georgia Brown).

- Place Names (St. Louis Blues, Sweet Home Alabama, Please Come to Boston).
- Day, Month, Number: Saturday Night's Alright For Fighting, See You In September, Three Times a Lady.

Sometimes titles present themselves. Penny Lane and Strawberry Fields Forever by the Beatles were derived from their childhood in Liverpool. A Hard Day's Night and Tomorrow Never Knows were off-hand remarks Ringo made that Lennon and McCartney appropriated for titles. And while these titles may have come across their radar without much effort, the important point is that the writers were paying attention to the screen.

Of course, sometimes they had to go looking for song ideas. When the Beatles wrote For the Benefit of Mr. Kite!, they created an entire song based on a poster for 19th century circus show. She's Leaving Home was based on a story in the Daily Mirror, and Martha My Dear is about McCartney's dog. When stuck for an idea, Lennon and McCartney were known to watch television, read a newspaper or just have a nap.

Another approach to coming up with titles is to set a timer, and in a similar way to Object Writing, dash off as many as possible within 5 minutes. By forcing yourself to work quickly, you'll prevent yourself from editing too soon, and will get out of your own way as you brainstorm.

Because so many of our best musical and lyrical ideas come at random times, often while in a social or public situation, lots of songwriters use their smart phones (some luddites still carry around a pencil and pad) to record ideas before they disappear, to be catalogued for later.

Since the title is usually a vital element of the lyrics and tone of the music, it's usually sung. The decision not to sing it should be taken with deliberation. This choice is frequently made for artistic reasons, although I have personally found few cases where I believe the decision was warranted. When the title doesn't make it into the lyrics, the performer often has an established fan base who will be motivated to learn the title. In other cases, it is because the song failed to come up with a line memorable enough to function as the title. If you feel your song's title merits being left out of the lyrics, be aware you are reducing its chances of being remembered.

A good title is a title worth repeating. For this reason it will most frequently appear in the Chorus or the Refrain, depending on which device is being used.

Try This

1. Do the exercise mentioned above. For 5 minutes, go hard and try to come up with as many titles as you can. No censoring or deliberating – just do it.

2. Do some research looking for titles. Any media outlet can provide inspiration. Or meditate, or just go on an artist's date and pay attention. Observe, inquire and become an active investigator of life's quirks, paradoxes, vagaries, truths and ironies. Look for what is interesting.

The First Line

Of almost equal importance to the title is the first line. This will be the first time the singer's voice is heard and the first chance to grab the listener's attention. Ideally, this line should set the tone for the rest of the song and make the listener want to keep listening. Many songs are better known by their opening line than by their title.

The techniques for finding titles apply here too. Remember that the imagination is looking for answers, simplicity and originality. It's up to you to set the scene, involve the senses and draw the listener in.

Because first lines can be so effective, some writers have a tendency to repeat them at the end of the song (this can also pertain to entire verses). They feel it adds weight to the opening idea, and bookends the song in a clever way. This can be true, but few cases truly justify this technique, and there are several good reasons for avoiding it. It can make writers look like they are clinging to their one good idea, and repeating it can seem like too much of a good thing. Unless the reiterated lines take on new meaning, it can be disrespectful to listeners, who have spent upwards of 3 or 4 minutes with your song, to have information they already know repeated for no apparent reason. From this standpoint, you are also doing your song a disservice – there are so few words to work with in most songs, why waste them?

Try This

1. For each of the titles you created, write at least one opening line.

2. *Imagine various scenarios* (as you may have done on your artist's date): the first encounter from a dating site matchup; a romance ending; returning from war; moving in to a first apartment, etc. Pick a scenario and distill its essence – what is important? What is the feeling associated with it? Now write a first line that will invite listeners in and make them want to find out what happens next.

3. *Go hard for 5 minutes and try to come up with as many first lines as you can, but this time, don't worry about tying them to a title* (they too may spark an idea for a song). No censoring or deliberating – just do it.

Verse Development

As we saw in our discussion of Structure, the Chorus and the Refrain are the sections where lyrics get repeated, and Verses and Pre-Choruses are where the lyrics advance. This is where a story gets told, characters are developed, situations get explored and the pathway to the Chorus's central message is paved.

All Verses and Pre-Choruses need to lead to the Chorus (the Refrain is implied here as well), and may colour the Chorus a little differently each time. Within the Verses themselves, each line needs to make sense and lead logically to the next one. This is where writers have to be vigilant and not presume that, because they understand what they're saying, others will, too. It's always worth a second look to make sure ideas have been expressed clearly.

To help make everything add up, writers frequently decide what has to be said before trying to figure out how to say it. It helps to lay out ideas in an order that the listener can understand, ensure they flow logically from one line to the next and guarantee all the key points get stated (and at the right time). Sometimes this involves working backward from the Chorus, and figuring out the points that need to be made to get there.

Before writing your Verses, try to be aware of what you want each one to accomplish (for this reason, song planning is a strategy many writers employ before actually writing a song – more on this later). Do the Verses need to reveal certain facts in a certain order? Will they establish Who, What, When, Where and Why (most first Verses do this)? What is the series of events necessary to tell the story/convey the message?

Of prime importance in all aspects of songwriting is keeping your listener interested. A good way to do this is to keep your lyrics moving forward, making each Verse do a different job. Avoid re-stating things from Verse to Verse (save the repetition for the Chorus).

A term for this most common of pitfalls is paraphrasing. Paraphrasing often happens because a first Verse was particularly inspired, but said everything that needed to be said, and the writer has nowhere left to go. As a result, the writer will unwittingly paraphrase the first verse in the second verse, finding new ways to say information already provided, but not advancing the lyrics and potentially stalling out the song.

Second Verse Curse

This problem of "what to do in Verse 2" is referred to as Second Verse

Curse, or Second Verse Hell. When you find yourself in Second Verse Hell, there are a few ways out. Start by asking where can you go from here? What could happen next? Is a backstory missing that should make its way in first, moving Verse 1 to Verse 2? Is there more than one main idea – could competing ideas be spread out over different Verses? Is there enough detail in the Verse? Could more be done to establish the scene or the characters, or create interest?

There's also the possibility that your Verse is actually a Chorus. Instinct may be your best judge, but consider whether you find this section more about message than about story, or whether it's particularly catchy, memorable, infectious and repeatable.

And of course, there is always Third Verse Curse. Unless your song strongly suggests it needs a third Verse, however, there are several possible solutions: replace it with a Bridge, replace it with a Solo, cut it in half or omit it and go straight to the Pre-Chorus (if there is one).

The song is too long

Sometimes the culprit is the structure itself, or the arrangement (are there unnecessary bars, interludes, repeated sections?). When the problem is too many Verses, it's time to get the eraser out. It's hard to be one's own editor, but it's all part of the job. It comes down to choosing what is essential for the song and finding ways to trim away what is superfluous. It usually also means finding new lines and rhymes, and it helps to believe that there's always a solution and you always have another, better, idea on its way (most pro songwriters really do believe this).

Try This

1. Using a title and a first line from the previous exercises, sketch out a plan for a song with 3 Verses, summarizing what each will do. Don't write the actual lines; just plan what each will accomplish to move the song forward.

For example:

Title: Your Shop is Never Open

V1: Every day I look inside (first line).
Singer routinely passes by the singee's store. He's interested, but it's closed even though it seems "ready for business."

V2: The singer takes an action to get the singee's attention. He demonstrates his interest, but the shop still doesn't open.

V3: He takes a bolder action, shows concern, declares his interest. Why won't the singee/the shop open?

2. Now write 3 Verses with 4 lines each. Use your first line to start the first Verse. The 4th line is the refrain/title. Use your chosen title at the end of each Verse, making it your Refrain (or hook).
For now, use a rhyme scheme of:

1. X (X indicates the line doesn't need to rhyme)
2. B
3. X
4. B (title)

Notice that lines 1 and 3 don't rhyme, but 2 and 4 do. This means you need to work backward from your title to find a line 2 that rhymes with it. Here's what I came up with for this exercise:

V1: Every day I look inside
I can see one light bulb glowing
Everything is in its place
But your shop is never open

V2: Yesterday when I came by
Knocked three times, just hoping
To be the very first one in line
But your shop is never open

V3: I'm leaving a note under your door
Cuz I wonder how you're coping
Someday I'd love to come inside
But your shop is never open

Be sure to make the rhythms of your lyrics line up with one another. Notice how these two 6-line Verses closely resemble each other for rhyme scheme (AABBCC) and meter (and they both end with the refrain):

I don't really hate you for doing me wrong
I don't really feel a need to be strong
I can't really say that my pillow needs drying
Cuz I can't say that I've been lying awake crying
I don't really miss you or your touch
What I'm really feeling is – not much

I'm not sad and lonely or hurting inside
I'm not losing weight or my nerves or my pride
I'm not going back on those cigarettes
Or making special trips to the liquor store yet
I know I ought to be all busted up
But what I'm really feeling is – not much

The Chorus

The Chorus is the song's calling card. If you're about to write a Chorus, put on your advertising executive's hat again. In what interesting, creative way can you sum up the point of your song? Remember, the Chorus has to work with each changing Verse, so you need to be careful how you manage the tense, the point of view and the message. Be careful not to make what happens in the Chorus a roadblock for subsequent Verses.

Try to keep your Chorus intact and unchanged whenever possible. This is important for a few reasons. First, the imagination favours a mix of the predictable and the new. The need for something new is accommodated in the changing lyrics of the Verses, in the arrangement and the performance. The need for predictability is satisfied by repetition in the melody (Verses and Choruses) and in the unchanging nature of the Chorus. Second, the Chorus is the main feature for most listeners (and most songs). To alter the Chorus makes the song less anchored and more forgettable.

There are times where the Chorus needs to be altered, depending on what happens in the story. In these cases, the closer the altered version can remain to the original, the better your song will be served. But bear in mind some writers and publishers believe a Chorus that needs to be altered is an unfinished one.

Rhyme

Why do lyrics rhyme, anyway? Do they have to?

Over time, poetry has largely freed itself from the constraint of having to rhyme, with the choice remaining an artistic one instead of a convention to be followed. So why do most lyrics still adhere to rhyme schemes?

The main reason rhyme is still an important feature of lyrics, even among writers who find rhyme anachronistic, is that it has musical value. When lyrics and music work well together, they create a third, more powerful, entity – the function of lyrics is inherently musical. In fact, a good lyric usually possesses a musicality independent of the music. Rhyme enhances the lyrical and rhythmic properties of the song and can create anticipation and resolution as well as variety and surprise. The musical effects of rhyme add to the overall impact, especially when the lyric is partnered with music that supports its underlying structure.

Rhyme is attractive to our ears and minds for two other reasons. It plays with our need for repetition – the delivery of an anticipated rhyme assures us that we understand what is going on, as well as our need for the unexpected – what will the rhyme be? How will it make sense and contribute to the rest of the lyric?

For most writers, rhyme is still a predominant consideration. However, striking the right balance of rhymed lines to non-rhymed lines can be tricky. Not enough rhyme, and the listener might have trouble remembering the song and identifying alternating sections. Along with the music, rhyme scheme delineates song structure, so if rhyme is minimal, it can affect the listener's perception of form. This can be mitigated by establishing a clear rhythmic cadence for each section and repeating it faithfully.

Then there is the lyric that rhymes too much. The worst offenders are songs where every line uses the same rhyme sound (it doesn't help when the lyrics are this banal):

> What was I to do
> I had to make it through
> But I was stuck like glue
> Yeah I was stuck on you
> Then out of the blue
> She appeared like morning dew
> She set me free – I knew
> I knew her love was true

The over-rhyming lyric gets even worse when the same rhyme sound is used throughout the entire song, making the level of predictability excruciating. To avoid excessive rhyming, be mindful that in symmetrical structures, like four line Verses, you rarely have to rhyme lines 1 and 3. For instance, a rhyme scheme of ABAB for a Verse can frenquently be replaced with XAXA. This eliminates the chance of over-rhyming (the example above could have benefited from this, rhyming only lines 2 with 4 and 6 with 8, or possibly only lines 3 with 4 and 7 with 8). Relaxing the rhyme scheme also frees the writer from the shackles of having to rhyme, opening up greater lyrical opportunities.

Another way to minimize predictability is to write an asymmetrical Verse with, for instance, five or nine lines. This effect is both musical and lyrical, and creates tension for the listener. Another technique is to delay the rhyme. A rhyme you expect to find on line 4 might sometimes be withheld until line 5, delivering a larger payoff when it finally does appear.

Another way to keep rhyme schemes and verse patterns fresh involves writing six lines instead of four or eight. Rhyme schemes that work well are AABCCB and AAABBB. In this format, try making the lengths of lines 3 and 6 contrast with the two lines preceding them. For instance: 2 Long + 1 Short or; 2 Short + 1 Long.

There are two basic types of rhyme, Perfect Rhyme and Family Rhyme.

Perfect Rhyme

In Perfect Rhyme:

- The vowel sounds are the same
- The consonants after the vowel sounds are also the same.

Classic examples include moon/June, call/fall, don't/won't.

A strong proponent of Perfect Rhyme was Broadway songwriter Stephen Sondheim. He defined Perfect Rhymes a little differently: "Two words or phrases whose final accented syllables sound alike except for the consonant sounds which precede them." Sondheim had great disdain for what he called "Identity" (where final syllables are identical – manic/Germanic) and Imperfect Rhyme (what most songwriters call Family Rhyme).

Most songwriters agree with him about "Identity." A rhyme like this one hits with, to quote Sondheim, a "muffled thud":

> The night ahead had just begun
> His business hand was on his gun.

Some of Sondheim's reasons for advocating Perfect Rhyme are legitimate. Principal among them is his belief that they help the musical theatre patron understand the lyrics better (especially upon first listen). His argument that Family Rhymes have less impact may also have merit, particularly when it comes to humour. But this is where I believe Musical Theatre and the Popular Song can diverge. Sondheim's main preoccupation is that anything less than Perfect Rhyme results in the dulling of the wit and a decline in the quality of songwriting.

Wit is, indeed, a staple of Musical Theatre writing. The sardonic, satirical and acerbic usually prevail over values more common to non-theatrical music like the conversational, authentic and insightful. However, an examination of lyrics from other forms of music will reveal that wit is not the sole domain of Musical Theatre, and that Perfect Rhyme is not required to facilitate a clever lyric.

Songwriters like Andrea Volpe point out that Perfect Rhyme can also appear obvious. Unrelenting Perfect Rhymes can make the listener distrust the writer, who may appear to be willing to contort or sacrifice the actual content of the lyrics in service to making the rhyme perfect.

The most important reason modern songwriters have no devotion to the Perfect Rhyme, however, is the limitations it imposes. If your goal is to express yourself in the most effective way possible, you need more alternatives than Perfect Rhyme can offer. Family Rhyme provides the alternatives.

Family Rhyme

With Family Rhyme:

- Vowel sounds are the same.
- Consonants after the vowel sounds are from the same **family**.

CONSONANT FAMILIES

In English, vowel sounds are few, but there are many ways to verbalize consonants. When searching for Family Rhyme, there is a hierarchy and order to finding the best rhymes, using the closest sounding consonants. The following is based on the work of Pat Pattison (*Writing Better Lyrics*) and on a cursory study of Phonetics and Phonology. Without getting into a full discussion of the mechanics of Speech Pathology, here's what you need to know.

For our purposes, consonants have 3 general categories: Plosives, Fricatives and Nasals. Plosives are the ones that "pop," drive audio engineers crazy and are the reason for "popper-stoppers" in recording studios. Fricatives use air to produce them and are characterized by a something of a "hissing" sound. Nasals, as you might expect, feature air passing through the nose. The difference in the 3 nasal sounds is determined by where the sound is stopped in the mouth.

Plosives	**Fricatives**	**Nasals**
Voiced b d g	v TH z zh j	m n ng
Unvoiced	p t k	f th s sh ch

Note: TH = that. th = faith

Note the difference between Voiced and Unvoiced consonants. If you feel your throat when you pronounce the sounds, you will understand why they are referred to this way. For instance, b, d and g can be felt resonating in the throat, while p, t and k are made with the mouth alone.

Rules:

1. Look for rhymes in the same category (Plosives, Fricatives, Nasals).
2. The less sound you add, the closer you stay to perfect rhyme.
3. In order of least sound added to the most:
    - Voiced Plosives (*ricochet, paid*)
    - Unvoiced Plosives (*free, treat*)
    - Voiced Fricatives (*fly, alive*)

- Unvoiced Fricatives (*faith, waif*)
- Nasals (*calm, wrong*)

What to do:
As an example, I'll use the word "broke." First, I get out my rhyming dictionary and go looking for Family Rhyme. Since it ends in a k sound, I'll look in the Plosive category. Since Voiced Plosives add the least sound, I'll start there, then move on to the Unvoiced Plosives. I'll only include words I could see myself using in a song.

Rhyme Word: Broke

obe	**ode**	**oag**	**ope**	**ote**
lobe	owed	rogue	cope	scapegoat
globe	code	vogue	grope	gloat
probe	flowed		mope	throat
robe	road		rope	wrote
strobe	showed		scope	vote
	sewed		slope	note
	load		tightrope	float

The context of your word will determine the choices you make, but this is a pretty good list of potential rhymes, especially when you consider the relatively short list of (usable) rhymes available with "broke" using Perfect Rhyme:

bloke	folk	stroke
choke	spoke	woke

Try This

1. Use the rules stated above to find as many rhymes as you can for these words: track, face, twin.

Remember that while the imagination may be looking for a rhyme in the places your rhyme scheme has stipulated they will occur, it is often forgiving with respect to the quality of rhyme if the rhyming words are far away from each other in time. In general terms, the further the distance between rhymes, the less perfect they need to be.

Types of Rhyme

Internal Rhyme

So far, we've been focusing on end rhymes, which occur at the conclusion of phrases and make up the bulk of rhymes you'll need as a songwriter. However, it can be very effective to use internal rhyme in songs with or instead of end rhyme.

Internal rhyme involves the rhyming of two or more words in a single musical phrase. Famous examples include the first 2 lines of I Am The Walrus (Beatles) and the last half of the Chorus of ABC (The Jackson 5).

Internal rhymes can be very useful for shaking things up rhythmically, and adding some interest.

It's a high time at the Oasis
They keep the lights real low
Hit the floor 'til you can take no more
Party until tomorrow

In the above example (XAXA), line 3 creates energy with its internal rhyme, and this also helps make the line more memorable.

Additive Rhyme (adds consonants)

- Vowel sounds are the same.
- One of the syllables adds extra consonants after the vowel.

Examples: see/been; feel/deals; tell/felt.

You can also add more consonants if there are already consonants after the vowel. Examples: street/sweets; dream/screamed.

You can also combine this with Family Rhyme.
Examples: dream/cleaned; club/floods.

Subtractive Rhyme (removes consonants)

This is the inverse of Additive Rhyme.

- Vowel sounds are the same.
- One of the syllables removes consonants after the vowel.

Examples: fast/class; bored/snore.

Assonance Rhyme (only the vowels match)

Assonance is the type of rhyme that can go furthest from its subject, and still retain the vowel sound itself. Consonants on each end are different (satisfied, trial) and only the vowel sound remains. Interestingly, this appears in a few well-worn proverbs:

> The early bird gets the worm.
> The squeaky wheel gets the grease.

Consonance Rhyme (only the consonants match)

In this case, only the consonant sounds repeat.

Examples: buddy/body, flush/flash, belly/bully.

Try This

1. Internal Rhyme: Try writing a few Internal Rhymes using this rhyme scheme:

Rhyme Scheme		*Example*
Internal Rhyme	A	*ready or not, don't get caught - it's nearly time*
Internal Rhyme	A	*lie in wait, anticipate - I'll give the sign*
Line	X	*a crime of opportunity*
Line	B	*a chance you have to take*
Internal Rhyme	X	*don't look back, when we attack*
Line	B	*and don't you dare (to) hesitate*

2. Find the following:

- 3 Additive Rhymes for the word "case."
- 3 Subtractive Rhymes for "realized."
- 3 Assonance Rhymes for "much."
- 3 Consonance Rhymes for "talk."

Spotlight Positions

As listeners, we tend to notice certain lines more if they are placed in strategic positions. For instance, writers focus on crafting the opening line because listeners pay keen attention to it. Many students of the popular song have observed that within the structure of songs are certain "spotlight positions" – slots in the matrix of the lyric where words get noticed. Armed with this knowledge, it's wise to ensure that what we say as songwriters is particularly well considered in these places.

The reasons for this are two-fold. Of primary importance is the musicality of the song itself. The lines that get noticed occur in places where the music gets noticed, too, and our life-long practice of listening to songs teaches even the casual listener to anticipate certain patterns and forms. The other factor at work is our natural pattern of speech. We tend to hear the opening line of conversation and the closing line best, with any irregularities and passionate moments also drawing attention.

Where are these places? Think of the song as being akin to a conversation. Spotlight positions tend to occur on the opening and closing lines of each section (Verse, Pre-Chorus, Chorus, Bridge) and in sections with irregularities and passionate "stand-out" moments.

In the case of the Verse, the first line is pivotal in setting things up and keeping things moving forward. The line just before the Chorus is often called the "trigger position," as it is so important for transitioning to the Chorus. In Verses of 4 lines, lines 1 and 4 are usually spotlight positions. In longer Verses, of say, 8 lines, the spotlight positions tend to be found in lines 1, 4, 5 and 8.

When it comes to Choruses, much depends on where you choose to place your title (or main hook) and how you've set up your rhyme scheme. Still, first and last lines are frequently spotlight positions, regardless of whether the title is found there. If you have chosen to place your title in the middle of the verse, this can be a spotlight position, too, and the music can do a lot to help make it work.

Repetition draws attention to the lyric, so Choruses and Bridges can offer a number of spotlight positions for the same line.

The Bridge is often the high point of the song emotionally and musically, so a well-placed lyric can be very strong here, with first and last lines typically getting the most attention.

Finally, odd-ball places will get attention – places where beats get added or dropped, extra lines are added, a build occurs, a modulation happens, a verse gets shortened, a spoken part appears,
music stops, etc.

Spotlight positions alone can often tell the tale. When the most important lines are placed in spotlight positions, you can understand the song from just these lines.

Example (I'm Driving by Stephen Maguire, Robert Walsh):
Feeling like it's time to go
Looking for an open road
Need time to myself
Need a little time to myself now
Got to the edge of town
Took one last look around
And I threw away the map
Don't know when I'll be back

Try This

1. Pick a subject and decide what events will happen in your song. Now map out what will happen in the spotlight positions. Notice that finished lyrics are not necessary at this stage. This is about which messages/ideas/narratives to say and where.

Example: Subject is Online Dating

Verse 1

Line 1:	**How I'm feeling (looking for love, discouraged).**
Line 2:	I've been to bars, grocery stores, speed dating, blind dates.
Line 3:	All I ever got was ____________ (something funny)
Line 4:	**Now I'm gonna try something new**

Chorus

Line 1:	**It's a brand new world**
Line 2:	going people shopping online
Line 3:	**It's a brand new world**
Line 4:	gonna embrace it cuz I'm ready for a
Line 5:	**brand new world**

You can continue doing this for the whole song.

2. Examine one of your existing songs to see if the information in the spotlight positions is working well or could be improved.

From Personal to Universal

It's common for songwriters to find motivation in real-life experiences, and want to raise awareness of an issue or try to make positive change by sharing the incident in song. The intention can be noble, but sometimes the experience doesn't translate well to song because its expression is too personal.

In her book *The Craft of Lyric Writing*, Sheila Davis advises songwriters to focus on writing lyrics that will speak for others as well as for oneself. She cites examples of students who wrote out their lyrics to portray events "as they actually happened," almost like diary entries. Instead of responding with empathy or support, the audience felt embarrassed – like overhearing a private therapy session.

The key to communicating difficult emotions and subjects is in filtering the experience so it will strike a common chord. A listener doesn't have to have had the actual experience to feel a connection and lean in, but they do have to relate to the meaning of the lyrics.

This requires the songwriter to dig deep and determine the essence of the experience. Can it be reduced to a single message, thought or word? What is the event really about for you and what is it you most want to sing/write about? Distill the circumstances and look for the universal truth contained therein. From this vantage point, you stand a much better chance of touching the heart of the listener. This means drawing a conclusion, adopting a point of view or an emotional attitude and taking a position.

This can render the original circumstances no longer relevant or useful, which can be difficult for the songwriter to accept. The actual events, however, sometimes get in the way of being able to make your point. It can be hard for songwriters to resist the need to cling to their personal story. Remember that everyone has a story – that's what helps you connect with others. Davis points out that when you fail to identify the larger context, you speak only for yourself and exclude the listener – keeping the lyric private, not universal.

Two steps to go from personal to universal:

1. Examine a personal experience and distill it to a single general thought, message or emotion.
2. Examine the circumstances and tailor them to illustrate and illuminate the above thought, message or emotion. If entirely new circumstances are required, so be it.

Try This

1. Take a deep breath, and write out the main details of a situation that is highly personal and has an emotional charge for you (this can be for your eyes only).

2. Now look closely at what is being triggered at the deepest levels.
For instance, having been cheated on by a lover may evoke betrayal. What does betrayal really mean to you? Does it mean you're unlovable? Does it mean you don't deserve respect? If not, why not? Does it come back to being unlovable? Does it spark anger? If so, why – because of a sense of injustice or disloyalty? Or if it triggers sadness, does it come back to not being good enough and unlovable? Whether it's anger or

sadness (or both), don't they both reduce to fear? Fear of being unwanted, of being unworthy, of not finding love? I see a theme here around fear, respect and love. In a word, I might describe it as "unlovable." Now – what is the song I want to write? Do I want to express the pain of feeling unlovable so others can relate? Or do I want to express anger and the choice to love and respect myself, and motivate others to do the same?

3. Take what you found, the central idea, and decide how you want to use that information. What will the central theme be used to say?

Lyrics – Use of Language

The Key of the Lyrics

Most of us are familiar with the idea that tonal music is written in specific keys. In general, the tonal centre of each key is its root note (or fundamental), and the way the rest of the scale notes follow (in terms of distance from one note to the next) defines the sound of the key. When chords are added by combining notes from the scale, the key takes on a distinct overall sound. Incredibly, as listeners, we have differing emotional reactions to the various types of scales, harmonies and keys used. For instance, a major key feels generally positive in nature, while a minor key conjures sadness, poignancy and drama; the wholetone scale creates an unstable feeling, and the Phrygian dominant scale can evoke either Spanish or Middle Eastern cultural associations.

When a note is played from outside the key, it often sounds wrong and breaks the mood of the music. With skill, however, composers intentionally use these "chromatic" notes to add interest or create an effect.

A similar phenomenon occurs with lyrics, and can explain why certain words or lines feel out of place. The key words of your song will create a lyrical tonality based on their direct meanings and the feelings and experiences associated with them.

Consider the word "plastic," for example. From an environmental point of view, this product has had disastrous implications, and images of sea creatures snared by plastic bags, mountains of plastic bottles and piles of disposed computers, phones and other technology come to mind. We think of how flimsy and cheap items like bumpers, toys and trinkets can be. We often hear "plastic" used to describe someone who appears artificial. On the other hand, this word also has positive connotations when it comes to the brain's plasticity (ability to re-wire itself). Since this positive association is not as common as the negative ones, however, it would probably feel like a "chromatic" note in most lyrical keys.

A good way to explore your key is to find other words associated with your "fundamental" (a thesaurus can be helpful here). Words like moulded, fabricated, false, synthetic, disposable, unnatural, cheap, trash would all fit within the key of Plastic. Words like authentic, valuable, cherish could also be within the key if used as antonyms. But such words as sorcery, witchcraft, divination and spell would clearly fall outside the key of Plastic.

In most cases, your song will have several key words, and they will all contribute to establishing the key of the lyrics. However, what if we combined two words that normally wouldn't have much to do with one another, like Drive-Through and Prophet, to get Drive-Through Prophet?

A few associations:

Drive-Through:	quick, cheap, convenient, low quality, minimum wage, bad intercom, unpretentious.
Prophet:	oracle, soothsayer, phony, divine, misunderstood, believer.

Now we have a much broader landscape and a richer key. Maybe a story takes shape about a drive-through worker who becomes known for his/her pearls of wisdom, dispensed with every order – the Drive-Through Prophet. Many of the associated words could help provide detail and establish the key. The tone could be irreverent, intriguing and revealing. Wisdom from an unlikely source. Enlightenment with fries. Quick, cheap, convenient oracle in a window. Phony or divine? So we see our key forming, with Drive-Through Prophet as its fundamental. Introducing words that evoke a serious and factual tone would be straying from the key.

Metaphor

You may have noticed that the Drive-Through Prophet is also a metaphor. The use of metaphor is a wonderful way to spice up your writing.

Metaphors portray a person, place, thing or action as being something else. They can tell us a great deal in little time, trim away unnecessary words and help us to see something in a new light. Monkey on my back; clear skies; smoking gun; soapbox; sacred cow; heart of gold; moral compass; witch hunt; whipping boy; night owl; early bird; the

Big Bang. These metaphors represent large ideas in few words. Metaphors almost always require some setup or explanation.

If I tried to create a parallel between love and a dog, here are 3 ways I might do it:

> Love is a dog;
> The dog of love;
> Love's dog.

Without context, none of these make much sense. This is where the lyrics surrounding the first iteration of your metaphor can help the listener understand.

Love never comes when I call it. Love is a dog.
He is a loyal and constant companion. He is the dog of love.
Love kicks me around and only offers me scraps. I'm love's dog.

One approach to creating descriptive language involves forming unlikely partnerships out of words, as happened with Drive-Through Prophet. By throwing words together, we can search for commonalities to see what meaning can be extracted.

See what happens if you select some interesting nouns, verbs, adjectives and adverbs and toss them at each other.

Nouns	Verbs	Adjectives	Adverbs
vision	scream	blurry	flawlessly
radio	insult	dirty	silently
the wind	spit	smelly	gleefully

Pair up a few words to see if anything interesting arises. Here are a few I came up with: dirty vision; (to) scream silently; radio spits (the hits); the wind insults her hair; gleefully smelly; flawlessly insulting; a blurry scream.

Another approach is to examine your main idea and make a note of its essential aspects and the images or beliefs attached to the idea. For instance, in the key of "train," train is the root, and some of the following words are in its key: powerful; slow to get going, slow to stop; runaway, adventure; on-time; escape; rhythmic; romantic, ticket, station.

Now consider what else has those characteristics.

Powerful:	emotion, love, muscles, ocean, strong-man, lion, nature.
Slow to start/stop:	passion, romance.
Adventure:	romance, pursuit of dreams, risk, freedom.
On-Time:	love (important events), watch, plans.
Escape:	freedom, renewal, change, amends, starting over.
Rhythmic:	beating heart, pulse, dancing, music.
Romantic:	adventure, escape, pursuit of dreams, renewal.

This triggered a few ideas: riding the train of freedom; her heart's a moving train, waiting at the station (will love be on-time? Will it take me where I want to go?); one-way ticket to starting over; his pulse is racing like a runaway train.

Try This

1. *Select a few ideas or subjects and see if you can create some interesting metaphors.* Let's try the words "fear" and "shadow."

> Fear is a shadow
> The shadow of fear
> Fear's shadow.

Now create a set of circumstances that can set up your metaphor or make sense of it (no pressure to rhyme – I just happened upon one).

For instance:

> His tie is his armour
> His smile is his sword
> But fear is his shadow
> The Chairman of the Board

2. *Pick a topic or main idea.* What is the key word for your topic? Now look that word up in a thesaurus, and write out any other words that appeal to you.

Is there a word from the above list, or perhaps an entirely new one associated with the main idea or key word? Return to the thesaurus and write out any other interesting words this search may yield.

Now see what happens if you put some of these words together. Do they have any commonalities that suggest an idea or direction?

3. Try writing out your own set of interesting nouns, verbs, adjectives and adverbs and see what kind of sparks fly when you slam some of them together.

Simile and other Figurative Language Devices

As most of us learned in school, the difference between metaphor and simile is that simile uses "like" or "as." One important difference with respect to songwriting, however, is how they each affect the subject.

If we take our metaphor "love is a dog," the actual identity of love gets transformed into a dog. Notice that the focus is now on "a dog" (because love = a dog).

If we take this metaphor and turn it into a simile, we get "love is like a dog." In this case, the spotlight remains on love because no new identity was created; a dog is something that is like love.

Metaphor is much stronger than simile and requires commitment.

Because simile leaves your primary subject unaltered, it can be particularly useful in a list:

Love is like a dog (simile)
Love is like the air (simile)
Love is like the sun dancing in your hair (simile)
Love just is. (summary statement)

Other Literary Devices

Lyric-writing also makes use of these devices.

Imagery:	descriptive language that paints pictures with words.
Onomatopoeia:	words that imitate sounds (boom, tick-tock).
Personification:	when a non-human subject is assigned human characteristics (a city that doesn't sleep, the stars dance).
Hyperbole:	exaggerated language (old as the hills, dying of shame).
Idiom:	an expression that can't be understood just from its wording (kick the bucket, out of the blue).
Alliteration:	the sound of the first consonant is repeated (Jumpin' Jive, Sexy Sadie).
Axiom:	Self-evident universally accepted truism (a leopard cannot change its spots).
Proverb:	Popular saying (a friend in need is a friend indeed).

Try This

1. Take the metaphors you created and adapt them into similes.

For example:

Metaphor: Fear is a shadow.

Simile: Fear is like a shadow.

2. Go through the list of other literary devices listed and write at least one example of each.

Verbs are Where the Action Is

In our discussion about Imagination, we talked about the need for action. Well, if you're looking for action, verbs are where you'll find it. Verbs energize and activate language. For this reason, writers often return to their lyrics and scan for verbs that can be supersized.

Consider how mundane these verbs are:

> My heart breaks when I think of you.
> She walked down Main Street in her little black dress.
> He drove out of town in his '68 Mustang.

Other, more evocative, possibilities might include:

> My heart *shatters/crumbles/goes silent,* when I think of you.
> She *strutted/skipped/sashayed* down Main Street in her little black dress.
> He *peeled/tore/limped* out of town in his '68 Mustang.

TRY THIS

Find some more active and interesting options for these common verbs and expressions:

> Go back to where you're from
> He cried when you left
> I'm looking for the words to say
> Falling in love

Managing Point of View

The point of view (POV) refers to the narrator's position in relation to what is being told or observed. The POV can influence the way we perceive the story.

The two most natural story-telling modes are first person and third person:

First Person (I) The storyteller is part of the action. This POV generally has the most impact because it's told by the person closest to the situation.

Third Person (he/she/it/they) The storyteller is not part of the action, but we learn about the characters and events through this outside voice. This POV is also referred to as the Omniscient Third Person, and the narrator knows everything about the characters and the story. Third Person allows the writer to "head-hop" from the thoughts of one character to another without difficulty.

OTHER POVs:

Second Person (you) This is also called direct address. The challenge here is that the narrator is constantly in the position of saying things to a person who already knows them. This can get tiresome quickly and can also take on a tone of blame.

One way it can work is as a substitute for Third Person Narrative, where the "you" who gets spoken to is really a substitute for "I". This is good for self-talk (i.e. "you idiot"), but is not really using Second Person in a strict sense.

Third Person Limited Omniscient As opposed to the Omniscient Third Person, the "Limited Omniscient" narrator knows everything about only one character or one side of the story, and all information must be funnelled through this one POV (no head-hopping).

Third Person Objective This POV is interested only in the facts, and draws all inferences and conclusions from the story's action and dialogue. This is a very detached, journalistic approach, and the narrator never divulges the feelings or thoughts of the characters. Because this is so clinical, it is not common. However, it could be used with great impact to present an undeniable body of evidence in an understated way (as in politically motivated songs).

As writers, we often assume that we are using the correct POV because that's what we started with. In some cases, a change in POV can have a dramatic effect.

As a case in point, I once co-wrote a song with a young woman who was the victim of sexual assault and wanted to write about the impact of the experience. We had gone through the steps of converting the lyric from personal to universal, but it still felt like the song was too hard to hear. By simply changing the POV from first person to third person, it added enough distance to take out some of the charge, and the song became more accessible as a result.

It's a good idea to run your lyrics through the three different scenarios (1st, 2nd, 3rd person), and see which one best suits your song. As an example, have a look at the song Evergreen (Andrea Menard, Robert Walsh) to see what happens when POV changes.

Evergreen – 1st person

The window in my parlour
Shines on my favourite chair
I sit and watch the season
Turn as white as my hair.
So many years older
A frosty pallor has touched my skin.
But I am a sapling
Inside a giant evergreen.
Evergreen. Evergreen.
Even in my winter years
I will be evergreen.
My brow has been moulded
With fear, and wonder and doubt
But I've softened at the edges.
My laugh lines spread out.
The voices of my youth
Still sing, sing with the river so clear.
The river and I are everlasting
We're both headed elsewhere
But we'll always be here.
Evergreen. Evergreen.
Even in my winter years
I will be evergreen.

Evergreen – 2nd person

The window in your parlour
Shines on your favourite chair
You sit and watch the season
Turn as white as your hair.
So many years older
A frosty pallor has touched your skin.
But you are a sapling
Inside a giant evergreen.
Evergreen. Evergreen.
Even in your winter years
You will be evergreen.
Your brow has been moulded
With fear, and wonder and doubt
But you've softened at the edges.
Your laugh lines spread out.
The voices of your youth
Still sing, sing with the river so clear.
The river and you are everlasting
You're both headed elsewhere
But you'll always be here.
Evergreen. Evergreen.
Even in your winter years
You will be evergreen.

Evergreen – 3rd person

The window in her parlour
Shines on her favourite chair
She sits and watches the season
Turn as white as her hair.
So many years older
A frosty pallor has touched her skin.
But she is a sapling
Inside a giant evergreen.
Evergreen. Evergreen.
Even in her winter years
She will be evergreen.
Her brow has been moulded
With fear, and wonder and doubt
But she's softened at the edges.
Her laugh lines spread out.
The voices of her youth
Still sing, sing with the river so clear.
The river and she are everlasting
They're both headed elsewhere
But they'll always be here.
Evergreen. Evergreen.
Even in her winter years
She will be evergreen.

Did you notice any advantages or disadvantages for the POVs? What choice would you have made (you can Google Andrea Menard – Evergreen to find out which one we went with)?

Try This

1. Try running one of your songs through different POVs. What works? What doesn't? Did you make the best choice?

Changing the Point of View

It's okay to change the POV during the course of a song, but if it is not handled well, it can confuse the listener. Try to be as clear as possible when doing this, making sure to use pronouns (I, you, he, she, they) to help signal the change and let the listener know who's talking (note: at the time of writing, there is a movement to increase the number of pronouns available to include all people, including those who do not identify with either gender).

The bigger problem is when writers change POV without being aware of it. A typical scenario goes like this: the verse is sung in 3rd person, and then the chorus switches to direct address (2nd person). No setup or follow-through is made to successfully make this change, and the writer often returns to the original POV without any transitional device. The result is confusion (who is the person being sung to?), and sometimes it can feel like two unrelated stories are being told. Because this is such a common problem, most seasoned songwriters are always on the lookout for it. It's a good idea to keep POV on a checklist of things to scan for in a first draft.

There can be compelling reasons to change POV. Frequently, it's done so the listener can see through someone else's eyes (pretty much a prerequisite in writing duets) or to provide information the writer might not otherwise be able to convey under the original POV. In literature and film, there are conventions (page breaks, change of angle) to convey the change. In songwriting, you have fewer options, so it becomes imperative to make use of your pronouns and clear language to indicate the shifting POV. Whenever possible, it's a good idea to keep to a single POV for each section to reduce the amount of head-hopping your listener has to do.

A problem songwriters run into when they change the POV in the verses is in how to treat the chorus. If the chorus has pronouns, they will need to change – it will no longer make sense to sing about "she," for instance, if the POV in the second verse changed to "I". A possible solution can involve simply removing pronouns altogether from your chorus so it will work with any POV. Here's an example:

> I'll run away to be alone
> I wanna hide myself and cry
> And taste the salty sting of tears before they dry.

Becomes (pronouns omitted):

> Run away to be alone
> Hide somewhere and cry
> Taste the salty sting of tears before they dry

In the above example, a slight alteration might need to be made musically, but in most cases, small changes like this can be easily worked out. In this example, it's not a problem because the words that are stressed (run away, hide, taste) still get the same emphasis.

Try This

1. Write a four-line chorus in the third person narrative. Now remove the pronouns to make it work with any POV.

Managing Tenses

Tense refers to whether the events or story occur in the past, present or future; verbs establish and control the tense.

As with point of view, consistency and clarity are key in communicating effectively with your listener. Songs that jump around in time can be extremely confusing. When a line is presented in one tense, and the following line shifts without warning, it leaves the listener puzzled and distracted. The time it takes to try to figure out what is going on is time lost and a barrier to your song. Here's an example:

> She was hard to recognize lying in that hospital bed
> She opens her eyes and smiles.

It is important to make sure the tenses (as well as the POV) line up for the entire song. In the course of a song, the verses will (hopefully) evolve and each iteration of the chorus or refrain will be arrived at from a different angle of entry, giving it a slightly altered meaning or attitude each time. When the chorus or refrain doesn't sound right the second or third time, it is usually because the tense or point of view has shifted, and what worked before no longer makes sense. For

POV, we explored eliminating pronouns to make choruses work with changing POVs. When it comes to making choruses (and refrains) more flexible, we have to manage the verbs to accept any tense.

Pat Pattison suggests 3 ways to manage your verbs:

1. Use the *ing* form of the verb, and omit any helping verbs (i.e: is, was, will be).
2. Use the *to* form of the verb (infinitive).
3. Omit verbs altogether.

Example:	she wanders like the wind she cries to feel the truth
Device	
ing:	wandering like the wind crying to feel the truth
to:	to wander like the wind to cry to feel the truth
omit verb:	a wanderer like the wind a cry to feel the truth

Notice that the pronoun was also omitted here.
Here's another example. This verse is written in 3 different tenses:

Past

She looked everywhere for something
Something she never had
A world she could believe in
A love that didn't go bad

Present

She's looking everywhere for something
Something she has never had
A world she can believe in
A love that doesn't go bad

Future

She'll look everywhere for something
Something she never had
A world she will believe in
A love that won't go bad

The chorus for the above verses has been modified using each of the 3 devices above:

"ing" Chorus

Wandering like the wind
Crying to feel the truth
Barely in her skin
Wandering like the wind

"to" Chorus

To wander like the wind
To cry to feel the truth
To barely be in her skin
To wander like the wind

"omit verb" Chorus

A wanderer like the wind
(with) A cry to feel the truth
Barely in her skin
A wanderer in the wind

Let's evaluate if the devices for making choruses work with changing tenses were effective. First read the past tense verse, and see if the "ing" chorus fits. Then try the present and future. Not bad – I think they all seem to work.

Now try the same thing with the "to" chorus. Hmm. I don't love it in this particular case, mostly because "to" could be construed as the reason for looking. The device, however, does work.

Finally, try the "omit verb" chorus. Not bad. It holds up across all 3 tenses.

More tools in the toolkit that may come in handy when your song is having a hard time making the chorus work across moving timelines and point of view.

Managing Clichés

Clichés are words and phrases that have been used so often that they're no longer interesting or effective. What might have started out as a colourful, inventive phrase, like *think outside the box, better than sliced bread or reinvent the wheel,* has been adopted so widely and used so indiscriminately that it has lost all impact. Clichés tend to annoy people, and can even create an impression the speaker is lazy. Some people just tune out when they hear a cliché – with the risk they will miss the point a songwriter is trying to make when they use one.

We all have our pet peeve clichés. Mine is "awesome". This unsuspecting word, which describes reverence, fear and admiration with a power no other word can, has been appropriated to prop up the mundane, and has been completely neutered by its over-use. It's a good illustration of how a powerful expression can quickly become a cliché, and just how radically de-sensitized to its original meaning people can become through exposure.

Clichés are well worn for a reason. At one time, they triggered a strong reaction and were considered original and amusing or interesting. A phrase is considered cliché when its power is waning. If you're wondering whether something is a cliché, it probably is, and you'd do well to avoid it. If necessary, use your "cliché-o-meter." I use mine to gauge my students' or co-writers' reaction to a lyric that I think could be crossing the line. I run the potential cliché by the group to see how high it registers, and in most cases, agreement is overwhelming about how far the cliché is pushing my imaginary needle. Most people have a shared sense of what is cliché, so it can be a good idea to simply ask. In music, there are certain clichés that are so ubiquitous they require special mention. Heart and soul, broken heart, playing games, deep inside, on my knees, cold as ice, love is blind, what can I say, angel from above, can't you see, walking down the street – these all register highly on the cliché-o-meter. The list goes on and on.

There are cliché rhymes, too: walk/talk, friend/end, love/above, touch/much, night/right, arms/charms, maybe/baby, eyes/realize, wrong/strong, fire/desire.

The songwriter's job is to find creative ways to say what needs to be said (and of course this gets harder as time goes on and more and more words and phrases become cliché). So create your own future clichés.

Clichés can, however, serve as excellent placeholders in your draft to hold an intention until you can find a better way to say it.

Finding Alternatives

Here are two ways to find alternatives to clichés.

1. Determine what the cliché means and replace it with key words. Look up the expression and highlight one or two key words that are either synonyms or key ingredients of its meaning. Then look up these key words in the thesaurus to find alternatives. Can you use any of the words you found to replace the cliché altogether?

Examples:

Cliché	**Key Words**	**Re-Written**
At the end of the day, it was all in vain	Ultimately, finally	**Ultimately, it was all in vain**
She was living with a broken heart	Despair, sorrow, grief	**She was living in despair**

Love is blind	not based in reason or awareness	**Love has no reason**

2. Decide whether you need the expression at all. Many clichés are padded with unnecessary words. Can the cliché be eliminated and still have the phrase make sense?

Cliché	Key Words	Omitted
I can't love you in any way, shape or form	under any circumstances	**I can't love you**
Tonight I'm your girlfriend for all intents & purposes	in all meaningful respects	**Tonight I'm your girlfriend**
At this point in time my options are open	now, currently	**My options are open**

Try This

Scan your songs for clichés, and try applying the techniques for alternatives.

1. Tweak a Cliché

A fun thing to do with clichés is to alter a few words to give new meaning or create a play on words. This is particularly effective for creating titles. Classic examples include:

Cliché	Title
Live and let live	Live and Let Die (McCartney)
Friends in high places	Friends in Low Places (Blackwell/Lee)
Break my heart	Un-Break My Heart (Braxton)
I'm not that kind of girl	(I'm) That Kind of Girl (Berg/Samoset)

2. Dig up a few clichés and mess around with them. See if you can come up with some interesting titles.

The Power of Word Associations – Saying More with Less

Details, specifics and action are tools that allow us to keep our finger on the trigger of the imagination. Simple, clear images create strong reactions. And with an average of only 200 to 300 words per song, songwriters are continually challenged to do more with less.

The quality of the words you choose can make a big difference. Words like "things", "just", and even "love" don't say much and need to be surrounded by stronger words or simply discarded altogether. Because the listener is trying to make sense of the melody, the arrangement/groove, and the lyrics all at once, there will be times when the concentration required to follow every nuance of the lyrics will lapse. This is especially true now that the average listener does very little active listening, and tends to consume music while doing something else like working, driving, cleaning or socializing.

Remember that listeners will react more to the associated meanings of the lyrics, and may misperceive the intended meaning. A case in point is the song Every Breath You Take by The Police. Sting's intention was to portray the singer as an obsessive and jealous lover, whose "watching" is akin to stalking. If you make the effort to listen actively, this is clear. However, the lyrics surrounding the tag line of "I'll be watching you" present positive associations to the unfocused listener, and the public generally understood this to be a love song (so much so that it was requested for years at weddings)!

Other examples abound. Springsteen's "Born In The USA" and Men at Work's "Down Under", construed as patriotic songs, are often played to get the crowd roused at public events. In fact, both are critical of their respective countries, but the public has paid attention only to the lines that sound patriotic, which, when combined with the mood of the two songs, resulted in their mass misinterpretation.

As songwriters, we need to be mindful that words come with associated meanings and assumptions the listener sometimes will default to. For example, the following words have several associations in the listener's mind:

Midnight: Shadowy, hidden, sexual, sensual, risky, adventurous, unrestrained, sneaky, unseen, wee hours, hedonistic, debauchery, unpredictable.

Light: Clarity, understanding, hope, warmth, divinity, the way, truth, brightness, sun.

Truck: Masculinity, traditional values, physical labour, cowboy culture, tough, cool, down to earth, country living, source of pride, rugged, fun.

Skyscraper: Urban, upwardly mobile, wealth, greed, power, faceless, landmark.

House: Home, hearth, refuge, sanctuary, castle, where I get to be myself, community, commitment, spirituality, privacy, achievement, family, belonging, turf.

Armed with this knowledge, the skilled songwriter can imply a great deal by tapping into the "culture" associated with the words they choose.

A line like "I jump in my truck at midnight" suggests a host of possibilities. "Jump" implies an energetic and enthusiastic attitude and probably a young person. "Truck" might suggest a rural person is talking, and they are cool, physical and looking for fun. "Midnight" suggests adventure, hedonism, unpredictability, sexuality.

That's a lot to convey in one short line, and a whole lot better than saying something like "I get in my vehicle today." By providing so much information in such a short time, the songwriter is freed up to use the remaining lines to greater advantage.

It's interesting to note that if the line were "I jump into my truck before last call," our assumptions would veer away from the sexual, and over to the picture of the singer drinking with friends.

Borrowing again from the list above, I think of a writer who wants to tell a story about how, no matter what's going on in their life or in the lives of others, home is a centre and spiritual sanctuary. They might say: "My house is a place to retreat and reconnect." Or, they might strip away some words, get a little more poetic and say: "There's always a light on in my house." "Always" suggests the eternal and unflinching; "light" suggests the divine, hope and finding one's way; "house" suggests one's personal temple, home and sanctuary.

Try This

1. Write out some of the thoughts, words, ideas and assumptions you associate with the following words: The road, flying, running, flowers, breath(ing), the ocean, clouds.

2. Find more concise and interesting ways to express these thoughts, and use words that tell more through their strong "cultural" associations.

I woke up this morning wondering how I got here.
I found you attractive from the moment I saw you.
I'm going to find a way to make you love me.

Sweating the Details

By now, I hope you've heard the message that with so few words to work with, you've got to make each one count. Be on the lookout for unnecessary words that take up space and dilute your message. This level of detail work will make a huge difference in the quality of your lyrics.

Toss Out What You Don't Need

These phrases include redundant words that can be eliminated: *Little* café, *very* original, *really* fantastic.

Delete or replace words that don't contribute:

His calendar's brimming with *lots* of work.

She strolled *leisurely*.

They raced *quickly*.

In *The Craft of Lyric Writing*, Sheila Davis talks about weeding out modifiers – getting rid of flabby adjectives and "ly" adverbs. What sometimes is expressed in 2 or more words can be condensed to one:

Heavy load	burden
Puzzling question	riddle
Large amount	lots
Far reaching	vast
Hidden reserves	stockpile
Talk quietly	murmur
Walk quickly	stride
Hit forcefully	strike
Spend extravagantly	splurge
Convey worry	fret

State the Positive

Any statement, expressed negatively, tends to have less impact than when it's stated positively – and this is even more true when music is added to the equation. It takes more words to say things negatively, a waste of valuable lyric space.

Scan for *isn't, don't, aren't* and *not* and turn negative into positive:

You're not happy	You're mad
I can't see	I'm blind
It wasn't useful	It was useless
She wasn't normal	She was strange
He couldn't find it	He lost it

Note: This applies to the body of the lyric, not titles (Don't Sleep in the Subway; Don't It Make My Brown Eyes Blue; Don't Blame Me).

Make Straightforward Statements

Songs are like 3-minute movies, not a weekly TV show that gives a "previously on … ." Provide all the facts, be direct.

Be Specific

The concrete beats out the abstract every time because tangible ideas produce a picture in the mind's eye. Abstract words – dreams, loneliness, emptiness, wanting, etc., leave a weak impression. In They Can't Take That Away From Me, the way she wore her hat, held her knife, are specific, expressing much more than if the narrator had said: "Those little things you used to do."

Show and Tell

"To define is to kill. To suggest is to create"

Mallarmé

The songwriter's goal is to engage the listener's imagination by showing instead of telling. To tell something is to give a factual account.

For instance, to say "she misses him" tells what's going on, but does little to garner interest or reveal much of any consequence. It names the emotion/situation instead of revealing it.

In contrast, "she goes to bed with his photograph" evokes a more vivid, nuanced and interesting picture. The visual aspect places us with her, in her bedroom and in the present tense. The photograph shows this is a close relationship, and triggers the imagination to ask why he's not there, about the precise nature of their relationship and whether he's coming back. In seven short words, the listener has been shown a relatively complex situation and the imagination is looking for more. In Rodgers & Hart's It Never Entered My Mind, the singer orders "orange juice for one," showing us he's on his own, and since orange juice is a symbol associated with breakfast, we have the further suggestion that he spent the night alone.

Good storytelling and good conversation incorporate a mix of showing and telling, so it's fine for lyrics to do some naming. This is especially true in choruses where, hopefully, the verse lyrics have developed interest and investment in the song, to the point where a simple and direct "telling" might be a good thing. But too much telling makes it hard to connect because the information comes off as factual and boring. So a good lyric usually features much more showing than telling.

On a more macro scale, great songwriting can also lead the listener to his or her own discoveries by revealing information instead of telling it. This application of "showing" allows the listener to arrive at his or her own conclusions and renders the effect much more memorable and powerful.

This is where I believe many religious and New Thought songs struggle*. Content is often based on beliefs and assumptions that followers of the same faith/beliefs share, but others may not. Little effort is made to bring new listeners to the same understanding, and the wider audience can feel excluded. And as for the followers, the presumed agreement around core beliefs and shared history makes the songs themselves uninteresting, as there are few "aha" moments. A similar phenomenon can occur with any song that forgoes the work necessary to lead the listener to realization. Instead, such songs offer slogan-like phrases lacking the momentum that results from the crystallization of a message, story or idea.

Remember, the imagination is hungry for details, and needs them to transform abstract ideas into clear and compelling images it can understand. So use specifics, simple language and action to show the imagination what you want it to see, and reveal the emotion behind the thought or action instead of just delivering "the news".

*In contrast are the mantra-style kirtana songs of the ancients, and the modern practitioners like Krishna Das. These devotional chants attempt to alter the consciousness of the listener, and usually surpass the 3-4 minute length of a church song allowing "participants" to alter their physical and emotional states, and the core messages to permeate deeply.

Melody

The painter has the canvas, the writer has the page and the filmmaker has the screen. In music, time is our canvas and sound is our brush.

Melody is one of the most important brushstrokes for a songwriter. Two elements define a song: Melody, the first half, is the "top line." It's what you sing, and what the second half, lyrics, are attached to.

Melody can be elusive to create and difficult to teach. Some melodies, like Over the Rainbow, Ode to Joy, Hallelujah and Unchained Melody are brilliant in a conspicuous way, and deconstructing them will confirm this. However, most melodies that get a foothold on the public's consciousness do so without such obvious distinction. And yet, we can usually tell them apart from "amateur" melodies that seem boring or disconnected. What elements are at work that make a melody succeed?

While melody can be tricky to both shape and evaluate, some principles and techniques appear often enough that we can use them to guide us, either as a starting point for creating melodies, or as an analytical tool to help determine why a melody might not be working, and what steps we might consider to help it.

What is melody?

Melody is a combination of melodic **motion** and **rhythm**, and stands independent of harmony, arrangement and production.

Motion can be expressed as the "shape" or "contour" of the melody. Rhythm refers to the movement of the melody.

When it comes to melody writing, everything is defined by what comes before and after. Choices are made in context and in relation to other choices, and the interplay between motion and rhythm is key.

These decisions affect the flow and the energy of the melody. For instance, a fluid, slow-moving verse can be contrasted with a more rhythmic chorus to inject vitality into the song; or a fast-moving verse might build tension that gets released in a chorus that features mostly held notes. These shifts in rhythm alter the energy of the melody and create interest. In a similar fashion, a rise in pitch almost always signals a rise in energy. So it makes sense for the most energetic part of the song (typically a chorus or refrain) to be higher in range than the verse.

Guidelines

Here are some guidelines when it comes to melody writing.

1. Stay Close to the Harmony

Most melodies will suggest chords that can be played with them. This is because the melody is frequently rooted in a key, and outlines harmonic possibilities by the way it is structured (i.e. how the notes are arranged. For instance, if the notes C, E and G appear closely together, this suggests a C Major chord).

Alternately, melodies that are created to match a chord progression generally rest on, or accentuate, notes that are found in the chords accompanying them, with non-chord tones being used as passing notes. Sometimes non-chord tones get accented on purpose, to create a "suspension" (this technique catches the ear and creates tension), but this off-balance state usually gets resolved by moving to a chord tone shortly thereafter. When notes get stressed that are not in the chords being played, it can sound incorrect or unfocused.

A goal in songwriting is to have your listener welcome the return of a part they like. This requires the songwriter to create sections that are distinct and interesting, which is why we so often see new chords introduced in new sections. This technique opens up the possibility of finding new melodic note choices to highlight or support the changes in harmony.

2. Range

There are several aspects to consider when it comes to range.

Effective Range of the Performer: When writing for singers (or instrumentalists), it is important to know the practical range that will sound good. Most singers can hit notes that extend beyond two octaves, but some of the low notes will be hard to hear with other musicians playing, some of the extended notes (high and low) can be difficult to hit in performance, and notes that exceed the singer's core range often don't sound very good and are impractical. For most voices, it's a good idea to write melodies that stay within an overall range of an octave and a half to two octaves. This will help ensure what you write can be sung effectively, because the range accesses the most useful and resonant parts of the voice. It is important to be familiar with an individual's range (and style) if you are writing for a specific person.

Range Within the Spectrum (SATB): Each singer's range will fall somewhere within the spectrum of human voices that are categorized into soprano, alto, tenor and bass (within this spectrum are further delineations, like mezzo-soprano, contralto, countertenor, baritone-bass). Knowing where a singer fits into this continuum will help you to understand your singer's voice and allow you to make informed choices when writing for their voice, or for a group of singers.

Range of Melody: When you control the range of the melody itself, you effectively control your song's energy. The higher one sings, the more energy is required and created, and this can always be heard and felt in the interpretation. Use this knowledge to your advantage. You will create interest and shift the melodic energy if you vary the range within a section, or from section to section. For instance, if you want the Chorus to have more impact than the Verse, go higher in range. If you want to bring the intensity down, go lower.

Most melodies have a climax. Normally, the approach is much longer than the descent, but this is determined by the interplay between tension and release in the melody. The more tension created to set up the climax, the more strongly it will be felt. You can probably think of a few other things in life that are analogous.

The highest note in the song is frequently found in the Bridge. This is because the Bridge is often the "break-out" part of the song, where emotion runs highest and energy is strongest.

Don't steal "money notes" from other sections. In other words, if the big dramatic, climactic note shows up in the Bridge, don't feature that note in preceding sections. You risk "giving away" the note (lessening its impact because you've used it already), and hitting the listener over the head with too much of a good thing.

3. Steps and Leaps

A step is a short distance from one note to another – from one scale degree to the next, and not greater than the distance of a whole tone. Larger intervals are considered leaps. Melodies generally feature more step-wise motion than leaps, especially in vocal melodies (it's much harder for the voice to leap around than, say, a piano). However, melodies that move only in step-wise motion can become boring, so to create interest and variety, leaps are needed. The larger the leap, the more it commands the ear's attention. They can effectively spice up a melody, but too many leaps can be odd, irritating and very hard to perform. A good balance between the two is key; generally, vocal melodies favour more step-wise motion than leaps.

If your melody feels stagnant, check whether it could use a few leaps to create interest. If it feels frenetic, see if there are too many leaps. Melodies tend to return to step-wise motion in the opposite direction after a leap or two. See the Mozart example on page 139 for an illustration of this.

4. Melodic Rhythm

The rhythm of a melody can be a key factor in shaping the energy of a song. Long, flowing melodies can be beautiful, but they can get boring quickly if there is no rhythmic drive to anchor them or bring them to life. In fact, rhythm is so key, there are songs that predominantly feature rhythm over melody (with very little melodic motion and a focus on rhythm), such as One Note Samba, Satisfaction and I Am the Walrus.

To create variety, sections will feature rhythmic melodic contrast within the body of a song. Think of how fluid and unhurried the melody is in the A Section of Over the Rainbow, and how the rhythm picks up significantly in the B Section. Likewise, in One Note Samba, the monotonic melody of the A Section is sharply contrasted in the B Section when the melody becomes very active and increases its range, moving quickly in scalar sequences.

Melodic rhythm works hand in hand with lyrics, and it is often the natural lilt of the lyrics that suggest a rhythm for the melody. Once a rhythmic pattern has been established, it is a challenge to find lyrics that will fit equally well without abandoning the rhythmic scheme. Slight deviations can usually pass without too much fuss, but if the melodic rhythm changes too much, the listener can have a sense of losing the melody, and the effectiveness of the song can be compromised (some publishers will not entertain the idea of deviating from patterns established in verses and choruses).

It is also interesting to note how often the rhythm of a melodic idea gets repeated as a foundational building block for the melody. An examination of most songs reveals that rhythmic ideas frequently get repeated, developed and used as catalysts for other ideas. Have a look at the Mozart example on page 139 for an illustration of this.

One way harmony can create interest is by varying the frequency with which chords change. For instance, if chords change every two bars in the Verse, maybe they could change every bar, or every 2 beats, or every 4 bars, in the Chorus. In the same way the frequency of chord changes can be altered, melody rhythms can be varied, too. Sometimes it is in contrast with the chord changes (i.e. a fast-moving melody with slow-moving chords), or in conjunction with them (i.e. fast-moving melody with fast-moving chords). Pay attention to what the harmony is doing – it might suggest melodic rhythms as well as melodies.

5. Alternate Where the Melody Enters

Sometimes when we write a song, we subconsciously keep repeating the same rhythmic ideas over and over. It's good to be on the lookout for too much rhythmic repetition in the melody, and to offer contrast to keep things interesting.

One common problem is when the melody starts each phrase at the same time. For instance, the first phrase starts on beat 1, and so do all subsequent phrases. This gets predictable but can be easily remedied by finding new places to have the melody enter. For instance, if lines one and two began on beat 2, try starting line three on beat 3. Or if the

Verse starts on beat 1 & ½, maybe the Chorus could start with an ⅛th note pickup (a pickup is also known as an anacrusis, and is defined as one or more stressed notes before the first bar line of a piece or passage).

6. Manage Your Endings

Another consideration is how phrases end. When it comes to melody, a phrase that ends on the root note of the key (the fundamental or tonic) is closed. It has a sense of finality, and is often reserved for the last note of a song. In contrast, a phrase that ends on any other note is an open ending, and conveys a sense that the melody may naturally continue.

The sense of being open or closed is heightened when you add harmony to the mix. A root note that is sung over a root chord (built on degree I of the key) at the end of a phrase is especially "final" sounding. It is the strongest closed ending because both the sung note and the chord are based on the root. When the root note is sung over a different harmony (i.e. the chord built on degree IV), the effect is less closed sounding.

When a chord-tone other than the root is sung over the root chord, the effect is open sounding. This is why songwriters often finish Choruses within the body of the song on a note other than the root, but conclude the final Chorus on the root.

A preponderance of closed endings can drag a song down, sometimes giving a feeling of frequent stops and starts, and lack of flow. If you feel your song might be suffering from this, check your endings.

7. Melodic Contour

Melodic contour describes the shape of a melody. This can be examined at a micro level – from phrase to phrase, or even within a phrase – or at a macro level to see how the melody evolves and moves through time over the course of each section, or the entire song.

At the level of the phrase, it's a good idea to change direction after 4 or 5 notes in the same direction. This will diversify the melody and sustain interest. It's good to incorporate both repetition and variation in the contour of your melody.

This is true at the level of a section (Verse, Chorus, etc.) as well. Consider the shape of the A-Section from Over the Rainbow (below).

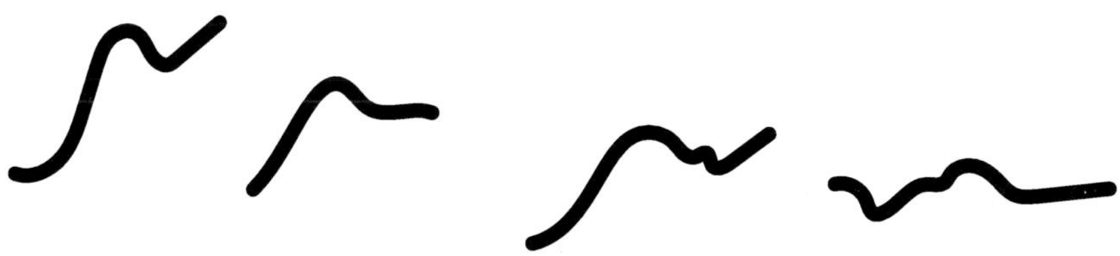

The opening phrase sets up the main idea – a leap up, followed by movement back down. The initial leap is the widest (an octave), and has the most emotion, as mirrored in the longing expressed in the lyric. The next phrase features a smaller leap (6th), and instead of climbing back up after it descends, it plateaus. The lyric here is more descriptive than emotional, and holding the last note opens the door wide for more to follow. The next phrase is very similar in contour to the first phrase, but starts lower (not as energetic as the first phrase), and features another leap of a 6th and a climb back up. This lyric is also more descriptive in nature than emotional and doesn't require the prominence of the first phrase's higher range. The fourth phrase offers a new contour that is less dramatic and ends the section calmly and in an introspective manner.

The general shape of the main idea (the first phrase) gets repeated two more times. And within the first three phrases, the leaps offer dramatic energy (the first phrase being the most dramatic, with the highest range and the widest leap), and resolve with a more neutral phrase. Examined over the course of the entire A-Section, tension was created at the beginning, with each subsequent phrase descending, yet featuring its own dramatic contour for a slow yet compelling descent toward resolution. Represented graphically, the overall arc of the melody is a quickly rising vertical line that then cascaded to its starting point.

The contour of each phrase was structured to build tension, release gradually and create flow. Repetition creates tension. The use of sequences (statement and response) establishes a conversational order.

Steps create stability and fluidity, while leaps add excitement and interest to the contour.

Interestingly, the melodic contour reflects the way the lyrics grab our attention with their opening expression of yearning, followed by several phrases describing what is being yearned for. The focus remains on the emotion, with less importance given to the descriptive lines.

Wolfgang Amadeus Mozart wrote some pretty good tunes. Let's look at one of his hits, Symphony #40, K550 to examine how he used some of the tools at his disposal. Here's the opening lick (note: if you don't read music, that's okay – look for how the melody notes rise and fall to create a shape and for how active the rhythm is):

Now let's deconstruct just this much to see what's going on.

At a macro level, we can see this melodic idea has two phrases (as in a conversation). Phrase 1 is the first 4 bars (starting at the pickup), followed by the second 4 bars (Phrase 2). Phrase 1 could be called the Antecedent and Phrase 2 the Consequent. Together, they form a Sequence.

Next, if we zoom in a little, we can see each of these two phrases is made of two smaller phrases, consisting of approximately two bars each. In other words, within the Antecedent phrase, we find two short phrases (or motifs), the first of which is the Antecedent and the second of which is the Consequent. Together, they also form a Sequence. The same thing happens in the Consequent phrase. This melody features one Sequence at the macro level, and two Sequences when we zoom in.

If we look at just the rhythmic pattern of the opening motif, we can see that Mozart repeated it in all four of the smaller phrases, making this the signature rhythmic "hook" of this melody. However, if we zoom in further on the opening motif, we can see that a smaller idea, a three-note "germ," is used to create the main idea.

This rhythmic germ gets repeated three times during the opening motif (creating tension), and is resolved with a single quarter note. This single three-note idea forms the basis for this entire melody, which gets expanded on throughout the piece.

It's also interesting to look at the shape of this melody. Notice how in Phrase 1, the Antecedent ends with a leap up. This is an interesting way to resolve the tension built up over three repetitions of the main germ, as the leap catches the ear and makes the listener wonder what is going to happen next. Since leaps are usually followed by step-wise motion in the opposite direction, it's not surprising to see that Phrase 2 heads downward, featuring scalar motion down to the next starting point a scale degree lower.

The next phrases (Phrases 3 and 4) emulate the patterns of Phrases 1 and 2, creating a welcome sense of repetition for the listener. They also offer variation in the way the notes change to accommodate the new harmonies, and features a chromatic note (F#) to inject some melodic interest and support the underlying harmony. Overall, we perceive the melody rising and falling, and repeating this pattern a degree lower. Represented graphically, it looks like this:

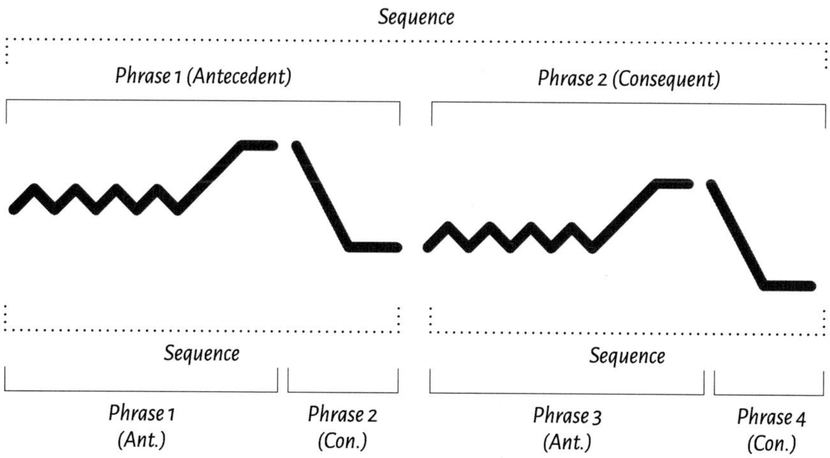

If you listen further to the piece, you'll see that the germ is used to create other rhythmic, melodic and harmonic ideas in the melody that follows, and that contrasting melodies help break away from the pattern that has been established, paving the way for a reiteration of it later. This juxtaposition of repetition with variation provides the listener a good balance to satisfy both a need for predictability and a desire for uncertainty.

Literal repetition (without variation) can also be a very useful technique, and we hear this a lot in styles like Blues, Rock and Pop. In many cases, it involves repeating a phrase verbatim, and following up with a new idea for the third phrase. This format is typical of traditional Blues forms:

Good morning people, I just landed in your town
Good morning people, I just landed in your town
I need to find someone to love, someone to help me settle down
(Memphis Slim – I Just Landed in Your Town).

Following the Lines

When writing melodies, many people simply improvise until they find something they like. However, there will be times when ideas are hard to find, or you want to try a different approach to break away from your usual habits. In these cases, it can be interesting to examine the chord progression you're working with and see what melodic lines are hiding in the chords.

This method involves selecting a starting note, and seeing what possibilities exist if you follow the chord progression using voice-leading. This means moving from your starting note to the closest chord-tone available to make the movement fluid. Keep doing this throughout the chord progression and see what happens. This usually means following the line using step-wise motion or staying on the same note if the note you're singing is common to the next chord (chords can share common tones). Once a melodic line has been identified, leaps and rhythm can be added later.

Let's use a simple chord progression to illustrate.

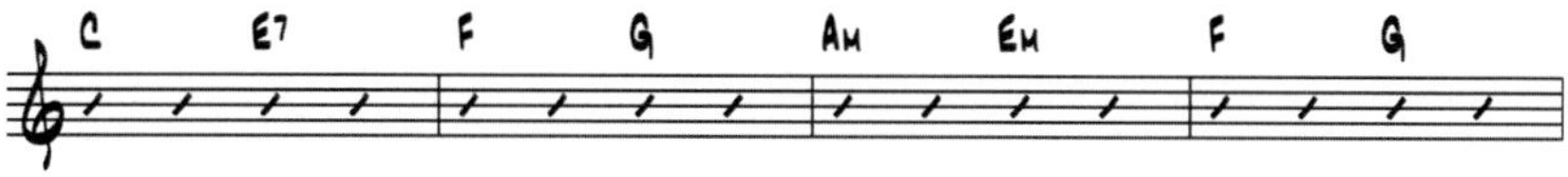

Next let's pick a starting note. For now, if it's a common tone, I'm going to repeat the note. Let's start on the root note, C, and see what happens. Here are just 2 possibilities:

Ex. 1 (Root)

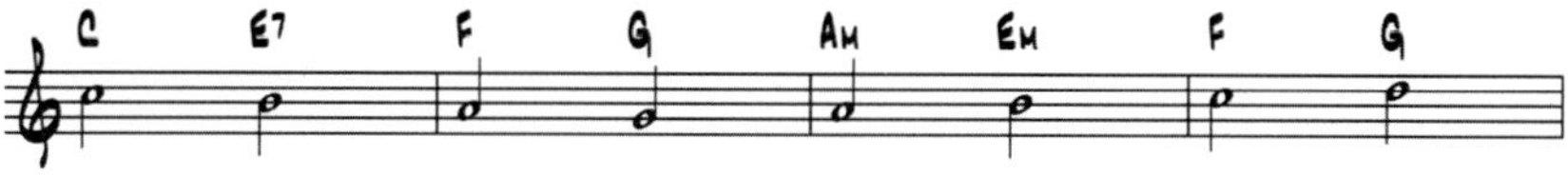

Ex. 2 (Root)

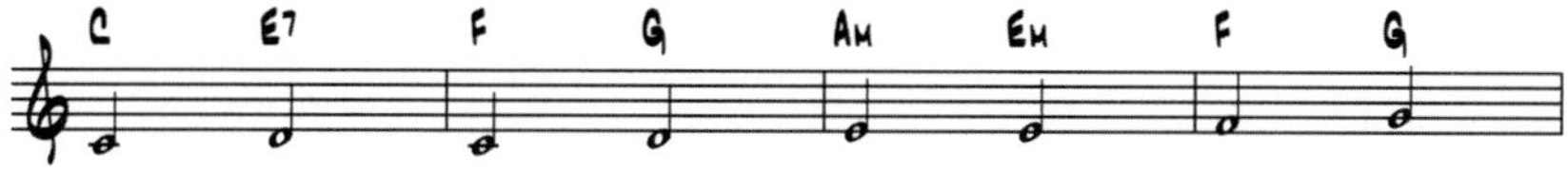

Let's do this again, this time starting on E (the 3rd of the C major) for Example 3, and the G (the 5th of C major) for Example 4.

Ex. 3 (3rd)

Ex. 4 (5th)

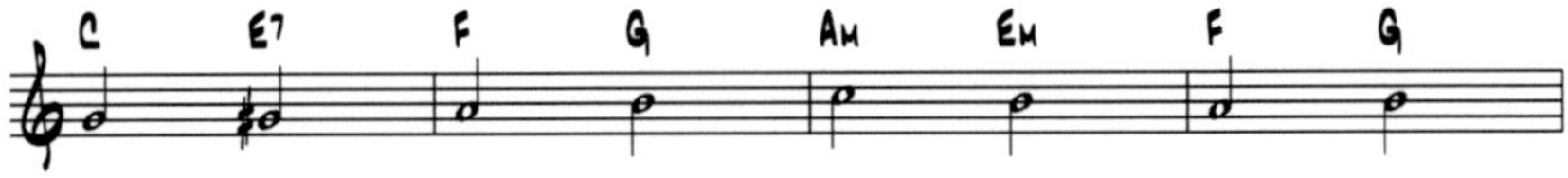

As some melodic lines have surfaced from the harmony, I can hear a few possibilities emerging. Now new elements can be added to create interest. I'll take Example 1 starting on C and embellish it. Note that all the notes from this example still appear where they originally did, but now with rhythmic motion and a few leaps between the original notes to create contour.

I'll try it once more, using Example 4, that started on G.

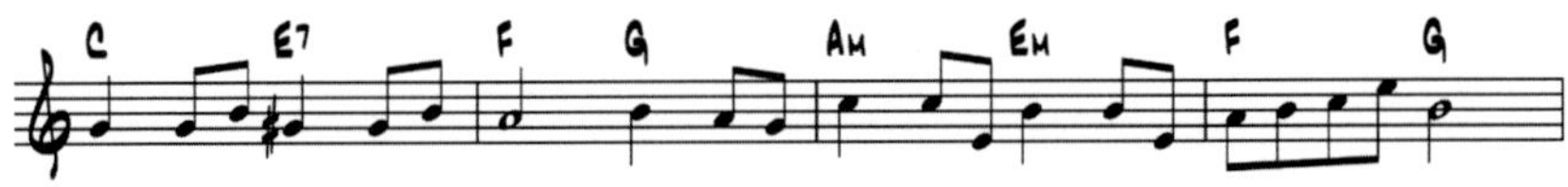

It is good to know where the common tones exist from chord to chord, and to know when notes need to change (and what notes they can change to when a new chord requires them to change). This allows you to either emphasize that a note remains common, or conversely, that it has to change. To illustrate, I'm going to establish a rhythmic and melodic pattern in this next example, and a) keep common tones wherever possible, and b) change notes whenever necessary.

In this example, the note C is emphasized, but some of the other notes had to change to accommodate the chord changes. However, if you know your theory (or have a good ear), you'll know that certain passing tones can replace some chord tones, especially if you want to create a line (or instrumental hook) that can be repeated. If we look at this example again, we can create a repeated figure that can be used over each chord:

In the next example, I'll offer two melodies based on the same chord progression. The first example emphasizes the use of common tones. The second avoids them.

Ex. Common Tones Emphasized

Ex. Common Tones Avoided

Knowing when to repeat common tone ideas and when to change the notes to accommodate chords allows you to use repetition effectively. Here is an example where the melody features common tones that work well over the first 3 chords and allows a repetitive idea to take hold. The idea has to change in the last bar, however, or it would sound wrong (and this also adds variation where it is needed to offset all the preceding repetition).

Ex. Common Tones Repeated

Phrasing

Phrasing refers to how melody is interpreted in terms of style, attitude, and emphasis. Most often we think of phrasing as a characteristic particular to singers, but the way a melody is constructed can greatly influence how it is phrased. The most important consideration is that the melody should sound musical, and of course, the text can play a significant role in this regard (with natural, believable, conversational lyrics). If the lyrics sound awkward, there's a good chance they won't sing well and the melody will sound awkward, too.

One of the ways to make your melody sound musical is to ensure the stresses that are natural to language are not violated by the music. This means placing emphasis on the right syllables, and presenting phrases in the way they are spoken, accentuating appropriate words and following the natural cadence and tone of the phrase.

Placing emphasis on the wrong syllables sounds bad:
How you do**ing**?
Bro**ther** can you spare **a** dime?
The presi**dent** fell down **the** stairs.

Accenting unimportant words can diminish lyrical impact and emphasizing the wrong syllables can make it hard to understand the lyrics. In Canada, the matter of phrasing is even more important in the French language, where syllables tend to get placed at the end of words instead of at the beginning, and where there is less of a history of contorting syllables in popular music.

One trend that is making it hard to understand lyrics involves the (over)use of melisma – a group of notes sung to one syllable of text. It has become a popular, if hackneyed, way for singers to display their prowess. When used for good, it can inject some soul and style into a performance, but when overdone it loses its effect and makes the words incomprehensible and the melody indistinguishable. When applying melisma to a lyric, try to select a word that has some significance (I/he/she/they/why/see, etc.) rather than a word like a, an, it, or the.

Try This

1. *Analyze Your Favourite Songs*

Go under the hood on some of your favourite songs to see what is happening with the melody.

- What is the melodic contour?
- How does the contour support other aspects of the song such as harmony and lyrics?
- How would you describe the melodic motion? When it changes, why does it?
- Are there any germs that form building blocks for the melody?
- How does the melody imply the harmony?

- How are steps and leaps being used?
- How are repetition and variation being used?
- What do you notice about the endings (closed vs. open)?

2. Exercise Using a Refrain

Try writing an AAA form song using a four-line pattern for each verse.

Make lines 1 and 3 use literal repetition in the melody.

Makc line 3 end on a different note than line 1.

Make line 4 different from the other lines, and place the Refrain of the song here for every verse.

3. Start with Contours

As an alternative approach to your melody writing, you could try designing a contour for each line to guide you in selecting the notes.

4. Exercise Using Verse/PreChorus/Chorus Form

Try writing a song using these criteria:

Verse:

- Repeat at least one musical line.
- Base the melody on a fluid, not-very-active rhythm.
- Use a generally static contour.
- End with an open ending.

PreChorus:

- Limit yourself to no more than 3 lines.
- Create an asymmetrical number of bars.
- Start the section with a new chord.
- Use a melody that features a few leaps.
- Make the contour rise at least a little from the Verse.
- Make the melody a little more active.
- End with an open ending.

Chorus:

- Use lots of repetition.
- Make the melody very rhythmic, rendering it the defining feature.
- Make the contour rise at least a little from the PreChorus.
- End with either an open or closed ending (very often the closed ending is reserved for the very last Chorus).

Now see what happens if you swap the approach for each section. In other words, try making your Verse the place where the melody is most active, the PreChorus is more fluid, and your Chorus features leaps (you'll probably want your contour to rise in each section, though). The idea is to make the sections distinct. Consider changing contours, range, rhythm, symmetry, harmony and use of repetition.

5. Follow the Line

Try "following the lines" as described on page 142. Start with a chord progression and select different starting points and different directions. Notice where the common tones are and where melody notes naturally move using good voice-leading. The line you find can provide a general outline for a melody, which can then be embellished with leaps, motifs and rhythmic motion.

A Word from Jason Blume

Jason Blume is a hit songwriter whose books and articles on the craft of songwriting I have admired for a long time. For this book, I asked Jason to offer some thoughts about songwriting he feels are important, and he kindly contributed the following.

The first time I pitched songs to a record label executive I learned a powerful lesson about melody. I played him my best song; a song I had worked hard on. I had slaved over the lyric, rewriting it until it was as strong as I could possibly make it. After listening to the first verse and chorus the A & R guy switched off the recording. I assumed he had heard enough to assess that my masterpiece was a smash hit waiting to happen. Instead, he said, "You've got enough words in this verse for an entire album, and I think you forgot about writing a melody!" That was my "light bulb" moment—the first time I grasped that melody was not there to simply contain my lyric; that I was writing *songs*, not poems. Of course, my words were important, but they would never be widely heard unless they were delivered to my listeners' hearts on the wings of unique, fresh, memorable melodies. It wasn't enough for my melodies to simply work with the chord changes with no "rub," no dissonance. They needed to be unique, fresh, and unforgettable.

I was a terrible guitarist, having mastered only a handful of chords--and I was an even worse keyboard player. But I realized the ability to write memorable melodies was an entirely different skill from being able to play an instrument or figure out the strongest chords to accompany my melodies. I decided to learn to play guitar better and to learn more chords. But in the interim, I was determined to not allow my limitations as a musician to constrain me from writing strong melodies.

I set down my guitar and began recording my melodies *a capella*, figuring out the chords afterwards. It seemed logical to focus on writing the catchiest *vocal melodies*—melodies the singers would sing—because no one walks down the street humming chord changes, beats, or bass lines. It's the *melody* that needs to stick in the brain, and that was something I could write.

When I was unable to figure out or play the chords I was hearing in my mind, I enlisted friends who were musicians to help pull them out of my head in exchange for twenty dollars or a pizza. In those instances, it was important to clarify that we were not collaborating. When I did collaborate, I chose cowriters who were more skilled in chords, grooves and harmony than I was—writers whose skills complemented mine. Some of my best collaborators were those who contributed musical backing tracks to which I wrote the topline—the vocal melodies and lyrics.

I analyzed successful songs in various genres and observed common denominators in their melodies—tools and techniques I could incorporate into my own writing. So, what lessons did the radio teach me?

Don't Be Too Wordy

A successful song can include lots of words, but only if those syllables and their corresponding notes contribute to a compelling, memorable melody. Avoid cramming in words and syllables if they compromise your melody. Melody has to rule.

Craft Melodies That Stand On Their Own

Giving more attention to chord progressions, drum patterns, guitar licks, and bass lines than to the melody that sits atop them is analogous to a builder spending the majority of his or her time and energy on a house's foundation, then haphazardly slapping together the actual home. The foundation is crucial—but not more important than the house.

Incorporate Fresh Rhythms in Your Vocal Melodies

One of the best ways to elevate songs from "good" to "WOW" is to write vocal melodies that incorporate fresh, hooky rhythms. This typically includes syncopation—placing the rhythmic accent on a "weak" beat—and it can be heard in countless hits. Regardless of your musical genre, including syncopation, and catchy, unique rhythms is one of the best tools you can use to help separate your songs from the competition.

Use Repetition, Repetition and Repetition

Your listeners cannot latch onto a melody and remember it if it keeps changing. I rarely observe more than two distinct melodic concepts within any given section (verse, pre-chorus, chorus, bridge) of a successful song. But when I critique work from developing writers, I sometimes hear songs that establish a melody (for example, a 2-bar motif)—then bring in a second melody; and then a third melody—all within an eight-bar section.

A sense of familiarity is sometimes achieved by establishing a melody in a short musical phrase then repeating that exact same melody. Other times it might be the rhythm that repeats—while the notes change. In other instances it might be a longer melodic phrase (i.e., 4 musical bars) that repeats. Listen to your favorite songs and you will likely hear the same rhythms, melodies and melodic motifs reiterated within each given section.

Include Contrast

Each section should be rhythmically and melodically distinct from the other parts of the song. In simple terms, you don't want the verses to sounds like the chorus, or the bridge to sound like either the verse or chorus. For example, if a pre-chorus is choppy and rhythmic as a result of including a barrage of short notes (such as eighth notes), the subsequent chorus might benefit from longer notes (such as whole notes). Conversely, a verse that relies heavily on long, held-out notes might be best followed by a chorus that incorporates shorter notes, for a more "rhythmic" feel.

Differentiate Your Chorus

Your listeners should have no doubt which section is the chorus. One of the most effective ways to announce the arrival of your chorus is to use higher notes. The chorus often includes the highest notes in the song, and in many instances, these notes appear in the first line of the chorus.

Another way to distinguish your chorus is to introduce rhythms that are not heard elsewhere within the song. Note that while many pop, country, and adult contemporary songs include choruses that "lift," urban, and urban-influenced pop songs often differentiate their choruses from their verses with a distinctly different rhythm—as opposed to soaring high notes.

Rewrite Melodies

What is the chance that the very first melody that pops into your head is such perfection that you couldn't possibly improve even one note or one chord—*even if your entire career were riding on doing so?*

To unearth your very best melodies, challenge yourself to rewrite each verse and chorus at least three times. Here are some concrete ways to rewrite a melody. You might place emphases on different syllables, words, or combinations of words. Explore different note choices—trying ascending or descending notes; experiment with different rhythms within the vocal melody—including long, legato notes, and choppier rhythms. You might also see how your melody works at different tempos.

Yet another way to craft alternate melodies is to repeat some of your syllables, words, or combinations of words. You might also try using nonsense syllables to create an added hook for the vocalist to sing. For example, "Oh, oh, oh," "Uh-oh," or "Hey, hey, hey."

You can also try a variety of different chords to accompany your melodies. Sometimes, a new way of harmonizing your melody can be just the ticket it needs to bring it to life.

In some instances, the first melody that flows from you will indeed capture the magic—but you can't be certain of that until you've tried to make it even stronger. After you've explored a variety of melodies you can always go back to your first—if that's the one you prefer.

Remember, there are reasons why some melodies stick in listeners' brains—and others fail to do so. Incorporate the tools and techniques that have proven effective in countless successful songs, but be sure to push the creative envelope and infuse your songs with elements that can come only from you.

Jason Blume's songs are on Grammy-nominated albums and have sold more than 50,000,000 copies. His name appears on the short list of writers who have had songs on the country, pop, and R&B charts simultaneously. Artists who have recorded Jason's songs include Britney Spears, the Backstreet Boys, the Gipsy Kings, Jesse McCartney, Hey Violet (debuted #1 on iTunes in five countries), and country stars including Collin Raye (6 cuts), the Oak Ridge Boys, and John Berry ("Change My Mind," a top-5 single that earned a BMI "Million-Aire" award for garnering more than one million airplays.) His most recent successes include three top-10 singles in Europe—all certified "Gold"—and a recent EDM release.

His songs have been included in films and TV shows including "Scrubs," "Friday Night Lights," "Assassination Games," Disney's "Kim Possible" and "First Kid," "Black or White," MTV's "The Next Big Thing" and "Taking the Stage," "MVP," "Dangerous Minds," "Kickin' It Old Skool," "The Guiding Light," and many more.

Jason authored three of the best selling songwriting books, 6 Steps to Songwriting Success, This Business of Songwriting, and Inside Songwriting (all published by Billboard Books). A regular contributor to BMI's MusicWorld and The Weekly magazines, he presented a master class at the Liverpool Institute for Performing Arts (founded by Sir Paul McCartney), and teaches songwriting throughout the U.S., Australia, New Zealand, Norway, Ireland, the U.K., Bermuda, Canada, and Jamaica.

After twelve years as a staff-writer for Zomba Music, Blume now runs Moondream Music Group. To read his songwriting tips, and for information about Jason's latest books, webinars, instructional audio CDs, song critiques and workshops, visit: www.jasonblume.com.

Process - Different Paths

There are as many ways to write a song as there are songwriters, and every song has its own path. In my case, there are songs I wrote in an hour and others that I didn't finish for 20 years. The magic of songwriting is that you never really know what's going to happen; it's like improvisation, but slowed down. Being creative in this way means you're never sure what you're doing. But if you can roll with this level of uncertainty, it's where you'll find the good stuff.

It's something of a paradox. You can study how to write songs, develop your technique in music and lyric writing and build your craft to the point where you can bank on it. But the creative process is messy, and it gets messier with each additional collaborator. So it helps to develop the things you can control to a professional level, but also to nurture the part of you that can allow a little chaos and unpredictability. When it comes to process, it means having one, but being flexible and open enough to take a different path if it presents itself.

Songwriting is a Whole-Person Activity

Songwriting is a process that can demand engagement from every part of our selves. The creative part of us taps into the subconscious, the mystery, that magical place where ideas are born and where we work until the well is dry. Then we take a break, and come back to the table with our intellect, and evaluate what we have. We identify the changes that need to be made, and then slip back into creative mode, finding inspired solutions to the issues identified by intellect. This process goes on, back and forth until the work is done. But we also engage a third element at various stages of creation – heart. The heart knows and reacts at a visceral level to the art being made, and is especially called upon when the music is performed.

In recent years, we've heard a lot about the different sides of our brains, and how the left side directs the more intellectual functions, while the right side is where the creative action happens. The science is still out on this (it appears the brain isn't quite so neatly divided; and women's brains access more diversified parts of the brain to make decisions than men's), but the brain does appear to have two distinct modes, and it'll suit our purposes to use the terms right brain and left brain.

In general terms, the right brain (RB) is where inspiration shows up, it's the wild child of creativity, impulse, daydreaming, wonder, and the ephemerally artistic. It has traditionally been associated with the feminine, mystery, emotion, spontaneity, intuition and the subconscious.

The left brain (LB) is analytical, critical, logical, orderly, specific and organizational and traditionally masculine. It's the rational older brother that keeps its younger sibling in check. It finds us a framework and context in which to live, and we need it in order to function in the world.

LBs are meticulous and often hand in great first drafts, while RBs often resist doing focus work before they get creative, and tend to think "feel" will get them through. Most of us are more inclined to one or the other, but over time, you can develop the weaker side and become a more balanced person – and this will pay off in a major way with your songwriting.

This is because songwriting requires both sides of your brain to get the work done. Once a creative idea takes hold, the process usually unfolds in bursts of creativity, followed by reflection and analysis, followed by more creativity and then more analysis, and so on until the work is complete. Sometimes this process takes hours, sometimes days, and even years. And that's why an open mind and a willingness to re-write are so important.

Our creative ideas are often inspired, and since we don't truly know much about where that inspiration comes from, we revere it. But sometimes we revere it too much, and are unwilling to question our ideas because we think they're heaven-sent. However, the intellect, while perhaps less attractive, is nonetheless as "divine" as the muse, and we need to trust all parts of ourselves and honour the process of creativity. This means following your inspiration until the tap is dry, but then allowing your inner analyst to have a peek and being honest with what it finds.

However, don't hand things over to the critic too soon or you'll never get anything done. This is paralyzing and will shut you down as a creator. A creative "safe zone" is required for everyone involved in the song, to facilitate expression of all ideas before analysis happens, and this will open the door for ideas to ping pong off one another and allow the best path to reveal itself. Stay in this creative incubator until the light fades out, and then take a break.

Over time, many writers learn to spot the signs of when creative juices have stopped flowing. For me, it's when I'm getting bogged down in minutiae, trying to solve problems that would be dealt with by a clear mind in 5 minutes. I feel a lack of energy, fogginess and a sense of coming out of a spell (songwriting can actually be in a form of hypnosis). This is when I put down the pen and go do something physical like walking the dog, do the dishes, etc. The idea is to disengage the right brain and give the subconscious mind a chance to regroup, find solutions and recharge. Studies have shown that one of the best ways to switch to the left brain is to perform a physical activity or task. It's not unlike the time when you can't find your keys and force yourself to look high and low for them, re-tracing the same steps over and over; but it's not until you've given up for a while that you magically remember where you put them. Over time you can come to trust that the solutions you need will show up if you let them. But when the creativity comes, you're going to eventually need your craftsmanship to recognize it and mould what you receive.

Brain-Shifting

In essence, we "shift brains" many times during the process of writing a song. Here's a typical scenario:

1.	Brainstorming for ideas	RB
2.	Organizing the elements	LB
3.	Creating the song	RB
4.	Evaluating the song	LB

5.	Re-writing/Problem Solving	RB
6.	Evaluating the changes	LB
7.	Re-writing/Problem Solving	RB
8.	Evaluating the changes	LB
9.	Finishing touches	LB/RB

As you can see, the process goes back and forth according to what the song you're writing is asking of you.

Heart

In all this talk of the brain, let's not forget the role of heart. This is a rather subjective concept that involves quieting the brain, and it refers to the trust, the instinct, the personal "knowing" we have as creators and critics of our work. It's what allows us to perceive when something feels right, sets out a path worth following, or dashes our excitement. It's the intuition that drives meaningful action, and it's an undervalued part of ourselves that tends to get disregarded in a left brain world. In some ways, this is the true domain of the artist, and it needs to be nurtured and protected. Without heart, you are without a centre, and will find yourself at the mercy of everyone else's opinions. As the expression goes, "stay in your head, you're dead."

Music First

In the creative process, many songwriters, especially instrumentalists, start with the music first. A groove, chord progression, melodic idea, instrumental riff – all of these can spark the imagination and set a tone that may suggest particular subjects, phrases and moods. For many songwriters, lyrical ideas come when they're messing around, playing some chords, inventing melodies.

When the music's there but the lyrics aren't flowing, many writers pull out their notebooks, files or laptops containing the song ideas they've collected for just this occasion. If you haven't made it a habit yet to write down your ideas, record them on a phone or catalogue them somehow, it's time to begin.

Melody Wins

When starting from scratch, bear in mind that in the war between music and lyrics, music is the reigning champion. Most people can think of a long list of songs with great music and bad lyrics that made it into the mass consciousness. There seem to be far fewer examples of good lyrics prevailing over dreadful music, and if anything, bad music seems to drag lyrics down like a boat anchor.

For this reason, many writers focus on the music first. They also know that a great melody can be dressed up in a multitude of ways, transcending trends and styles, and get passed down through generations. Songs like Crazy, Hallelujah, I Heard It Through the Grapevine, Fever, Landslide and Yesterday have enduring melodies that led to these songs being covered by many artists in many ways for many years. They are eminently "singable." Thus, many songwriters feel melody should be the top priority.

The singability of the melody trumps the cleverness of the lyric (almost) every time. Melody wins. It's that simple. I've seen students bring in songs with captivating arrangements but melodies that were clearly written on an instrument. They had too much movement, too many leaps, too wide a range, too many non-chord tones, and generally lacked the characteristics of a good vocal melody. They were not singable, and it took every ounce of the singer's skill to make them sound any good at all. It's hard to write well for voice if you yourself don't sing, at least a little. So if you're someone who's writing for others, it would be a good goal to seek a vocal coach to get your singing to a level where you can at least sing your own melodies. It will change the way you write.

Similarly, I've had students present songs with brilliant lyrics but uninteresting, meandering, or confused melodies that served to block the listener from hearing the lyrics. If your melody is solid, you can do a great deal with it lyrically and interpretively.

Even though Melody wins, Lyrics are contenders: great lyrics can change lives, unite people and reveal important truths. Their power should not be underestimated. The test of a great song is whether both aspects of music and lyrics stand the test of time, and it's why, in my opinion, a song like Moon River will endure longer than Hallelujah.

When a melody does emerge, a good question to ask is: Does this feel like a verse or a chorus? More often than not, your instinct will answer. But if you're not sure, remember the general features that differentiate Verses from Choruses. Verses move information, so they focus less on repetition. Choruses usually have more energy than verses and bring your point home. Does your melody sound or feel like it's disclosing something, or is it the culmination of something? Is it the unfolding of an idea or a rallying cry?

Hooks

Another great musical starting point is the Hook. If you listen to classic rock songs like Satisfaction, Day Tripper, Pretty Woman, Walk This Way and American Woman, it's clear the real hook is the main guitar riff. In the case of Satisfaction, the melody consists of 3 notes. These songs were built on the hook.

Note: Because the legal definition of a song most often involves only lyrics and melody, these hooks are usually considered part of the arrangement, and this contribution may not actually form part of the song.

Main Hooks

More often, however, the main hook is a melodic idea, and instrumental licks are considered Secondary Hooks. Main (or Primary) Hooks usually feature the title, are repeated prominently, can be found in the chorus, and have the strongest impact. Love 'em or hate 'em, think of how memorable the choruses to these songs are: Who Let The Dogs Out; Gangsta's Paradise; Whip It; Bad Romance; Call Me Maybe; Don't You Want Me; Stayin' Alive; Stop In The Name of Love; Sweet Caroline; Wannabe; Should I Stay Or Should I Go; I Love Rock and Roll; Happy; Ring of Fire; Beat It; No Woman No Cry; Achy Breaky Heart; Empire State of Mind; Guitars Cadillacs; Don't Stop Believin'; Pride (In The Name of Love); Crazy; Highway To Hell.

Secondary Hooks

Very often, Secondary Hooks, whether played or sung, have the same characteristics as the Main Hook, but in the context of the song are simply not THE hook. Secondary hooks may be prominent backups that everyone remembers, instrumental riffs that become ear worms, or an inventive drum pattern, but they're all supporting players to the Main Hook.

For a study in contrasting Primary and Secondary Hooks, check out Shake It Off (Taylor Swift), Money For Nothing (Dire Straits), All About That Bass (Meaghan Trainor), My Girl (The Temptations); Your Body Is a Wonderland (John Mayer); Life Is A Highway (Tom Cochrane) and Love Shack (The B-52's).

Sneaky Hooks

"Sneaky Hooks" is the term I'm using for those signature parts of a song that are not heavily featured Primary or Secondary Hooks, but are important nonetheless. Bass lines figure prominently here – usually as foundational elements. Think of Midnight Hour (Wilson Pickett, Roxy Music, The Commitments), Radar Love (Golden Earring), I Wish (Stevie Wonder), Money (Pink Floyd), Walking on The Moon (The Police) and almost anything James Jamerson ever played on. Other hooks include special effects like the talk-box (Peter Frampton), slide guitar glissandi (Steve Miller), autotune (Cher et al), memorable solos (Reelin' In The Years, Midnight at the Oasis, Just the Way You Are), and all manner of drum fills, stops and changeups (like dropped or added beats or changes in feel).

The Groove

For some music-first writers, a chord progression or a melody will get them started. For others, drum beats and loops get a groove going and they build from there. For certain styles like Pop, R&B and Rap, which focus so much on the groove, it makes good sense to start with the beat.

The groove, or beat, has been a defining feature of music for ages. For instance, we think of classical music as concert hall repertoire, but much of it was originally written for dancing. The Allemande, Bolero, Bourée, Mazurka, Gavotte, Hornpipe, Tarantella, Minuet, Polka, Waltz, Gigue and Tango were all dance forms, defined by a particular type of beat.

In *The Billboard Guide To Writing And Producing Songs That Sell,* Eric Beall states: "In many ways, the story of popular music in America easily could be traced through the evolution of rhythm." From the Blues to Ragtime to the Jitterbug to Jazz/Swing to Surf to Metal to Line Dancing to Vogueing and beyond, each era has been defined by its beats and its dances. With the advent of radio and television shows like American Bandstand, kids were seen boogying to the latest dance crazes like The Twist, The Locomotion and the Mashed Potato, and the Beatles became famous for their infectious "Mersey Beat." Motown added a soulful groove to the mix, and styles like Disco, Punk, New Wave and Hip Hop all changed the way people moved. Rhythm is a powerful tool for making direct connection with an audience.

This tool has never been more important. With access to recording equipment so ubiquitous, and the booming DIY trend, the market has been flooded with more music than ever, and it's hard to break through the static. At the same time, people are distracted by technology, constantly multi-tasking and living life at an ever-quickening pace. If your song is taking too long to make an impression, today's listener will move on, usually within seconds. This is where a great groove can grab someone's attention and hold it until the other brilliant elements of your song have had a chance to be heard.

Rhythm doesn't hit at the level of intellect. It's a visceral, physical, even primal thing. It doesn't challenge listeners to speculate about meaning or try to decipher a melody. It makes people feel, and the reaction is immediate.

Most songs, especially the ones that get played on radio, are in 4/4, and have a backbeat. So, what separates one groove from another? Why do some songs just feel better than others?

First of all, rhythm and groove are about more than just a beat. Two different drummers can play the same part, but one will feel better than the other. Sometimes it's a matter of attitude coming through the instrument, or a level of skill that elevates performance, or a strong sense of rhythm, or excellent interpretive skills.

But it's also about energy. And energy transcends tempo. A ballad can have as much intensity as a fast song, and the weight of certain slow and mid-tempo grooves is what helps define a style like Rap or Rock.

Energy can be felt at the individual level. John Bonham brought a whole lot more physical energy to the music than, say, a jazz drummer like Philly Joe Jones. But Philly Joe brought a kind of cool energy – an improvisational intensity that sets an entirely different kind of groove. Each player brings their individuality, and hence personal energy, that shows up in their playing. But groups also have an energy that feeds off each individual to create the whole. With great musicians, you can hear and feel the shifts in group dynamics, and this creates excitement and elevates the groove.

In the days when records were made with all real musicians, it was about how people played together and the combination of their unique sound, feel, connectedness and creativity. It was about that special "jam" – the way a Bernard Purdie, Steve Gadd or Vinnie Colaiuta would "lay it down." The special feel of bass players like James Jamerson, Bootsy Collins, Pino Palladino, Leland Sklar and Flea. The beautiful (yet sometimes imperfect) ways rhythm sections would lock in together – Sly Dunbar and Robbie Shakespeare, Charlie Watts and Bill Wyman, Ringo Starr and Paul McCartney, Sting and Stewart Copeland, Tony Thompson and Bernard Edwards, Mitch Mitchell and Noel Redding, Hal Blaine and Carol Kaye, John Bonham and John Paul Jones. What these musicians brought to the table was artistry and the intangible human qualities of grit, elegance and musicality. The energy that emerged from these players helped define the feel and identity of the music they made, and this is why artists and producers still take the time and bear the expense of recording real musicians.

And, of course, there are all the other elements that contribute to the groove – funky guitar parts, percussive and rhythmic vocals, hooky keyboard parts, etc. How all these ideas combine to build energy, whether to create a danceable beat or make a slow ballad sit, forms a unified feeling in the same way a chef mixes ingredients to make a unique meal.

In today's Pop, R&B and Rap scenes, however, real musicians have been largely replaced by samples and a focus on production. In fact, the use of real musicians would seem anachronistic in some contexts. What this approach loses in humanity, however, can be compensated for with interesting sounds and arrangements.

Since the focus has swung so heavily toward production, the producer has become, if not king, then certainly king-maker. And this is why songwriters now need to learn about production techniques. Thankfully, it's much easier and cheaper to create grooves with samples than it is to master your craft as a musician or hire and direct those who have. Almost all such work is done with Midi and this allows the producer/songwriter to mess around for an unlimited time to find samples, parts and sounds that will make the groove come alive.

Current technology allows for some extremely innovative sound creation. Ironically, however, some of the early digital sounds that marked the '80s and '90s, like the Roland TR-808 drum machine and certain string sounds and other synth patches, are back in style with some musicians (despite being discarded by many who had to actually use these sounds in the early days). Technology also allows music to be more aggressive (think of the ultra-low, gut rumbling kick and bass notes, and extreme mastering levels), and this, too, creates energy. Any groove that has energy and aggressiveness will build momentum, regardless of tempo or style.

Recycled Grooves

When it comes to commercial music, a popular beat can go out of style overnight and quickly date the sound of the music. After World War I, Jazz became popular music, and the Charleston was the Flapper generation's dance of choice. But this all changed when the Depression hit. Similarly, the Twist was all the rage in 1960, but was passé by 1965. Surf, Disco, Punk – the list goes on of styles that have come and gone. But along the way they became linked forever to the eras when they were popular. This is good to know if you're called on to write something that evokes a historical sound – the quickest way to summon up the music of another era is through rhythm.

Musical styles, however, often enjoy a comeback a few decades after they fell from grace, as evidenced by the number of songs that have borrowed grooves from previous generations and added contemporary production values.

One of the classics is the "Bo Diddley" groove. This rhythmic pattern has found its way into hundreds of songs, including I Want Candy (Bow Wow Wow), Faith (George Michael), Love is a Battlefield (Pat Benatar), Who Do You Love (George Thoroughgood), She's the One (Bruce Springsteen), Desire (U2), Lover's Walk (Elvis Costello) and Not Fade Away (The Rolling Stones).

The "re-purposing" goes on: Christina Aguilera's Candyman is a tip of the hat to the Andrews Sisters' Boogie Woogie Bugle Boy. Amy Winehouse recycled the sounds and feel of 1960's London. The Ramones, The Sex Pistols and other punk bands took '50s and '60s grooves and added attitude. Loreena McKennitt was influenced by Celtic and Middle Eastern traditions. Prince borrowed heavily from the James Brown playbook, and Robin Thicke and Pharrell imitated Marvin Gaye's Got To Give It Up (unfortunately they got sued for it. Most industry people feel they shouldn't have though, because, at least until that decision, you couldn't copyright a groove).

Grooves sometimes find themselves in odd places. Some artists blend unlikely grooves into their music to create interesting new sounds. Dido use chilled out club beats to distinguish her style. The Bee Gees were folk stars before they became disco icons. Nelly Furtado and Gwen Stefani borrowed hip-hop beats to create their Pop sounds. David Bowie borrowed from every style he encountered. Country went Rock. So did Jazz. R&B went Pop.

Try This

1. Grab an instrument and pick a chord progression. If you're stuck, steal one from another song. Use this to prompt ideas, especially melodic ones.

2. Use a drum machine, loop station, actual drums or just your hands on a guitar back. Mess around with a groove as the starting point and see what happens.

Lyrics First

There are several situations where you might need to write from Lyrics. Some songwriters naturally start with lyrics, or are inspired by a line or an idea that provides the spark. But sometimes lyrics come first because they have been handed to you.

Lyrics Provided

When lyrics are provided, your main challenge is to find a mood that suits them, emphasize the important lines, and tailor a melody that will showcase the lyrics in interesting ways. This work is more compositional in nature, and commonly happens when a writer is tasked with writing the music to a musical, completing a song for a specific purpose, or given lyrics to build a song around (for a song or a commercial).

Your talents as a lyricist will still come into play as you analyze the words for what to focus on for creating refrains and choruses, what rhythms the lyric suggests, and ways to improve phrasing by making small changes. When writing a musical, you'll also want to sit down with the playwright to see what the vision is for the overall work so you can make sure the music provides the necessary emotional support for the piece. What does each song need to achieve in meaning, intensity and moving the story forward? You'll need to ensure the music is written so the lyrics can be clearly understood and the points that need to be made hit their mark.

I once wrote a musical with a playwright from another city. He would send me the lyrics and I would ask for cuts. He was a non-musician with a good sense of rhythm in his lyrics, but a poor sense of the brevity necessary in songwriting. Thankfully, he was open to suggestion, but I still had to find creative ways to incorporate all his lyrics into song. I would send him demos of what I came up with and he would send me his responses. This worked quite well, but it's still easier to write with someone in the same town where you can get in the same room together (although technology like Skype and Facetime are mitigating this problem to a large degree). In all collaborations, communication is key to getting the results that will satisfy you both.

This is also true when tasked with writing a song for a special occasion or adding music to existing lyrics. It's best not to assume what the lyricist wants from the music, so make sure you talk about what the end goal is. This shows respect and will also help avoid working toward the wrong objective and then re-doing your work.

Starting from the Subject

There are times when you know what the subject matter is that you need to write about (and times when you just need to find something, anything, to write about).

From The Trenches

Whenever I've written songs on commission, I've always had extensive discussion with the client and my collaborators to make 100% sure we all knew what our mission was. When working on a song for an internationally recognized organization for social change, my co-writer and I received about 5 pages worth of descriptions from the client about what he wanted in the song. This included some enthusiastic suggestions of particularly hackneyed and banal lines that I was eager to avoid. After several meetings with my co-writer and many emails back and forth to our client in a foreign country (and a little international diplomacy to side-step the lyric suggestions), we finally narrowed down our mission to a few key points and delivered a much more coherent and succinct song than we would have otherwise.

When writing to someone else's agenda, it's worth the time and patience to ask all the questions necessary until you feel absolutely clear about what you have been tasked to do. Further, a quick email recap of your conversations to all stakeholders keeps lines of communication clear, and helps replace assumptions with assertions. It's worth noting that even with the best communication, and despite providing exactly what was asked for, clients can be capricious and still turn down your work.

Starting from Scratch

Most of the time, however, songwriters aren't working to complete a specific mission. More commonly they find themselves wondering "what should I write about?"

To answer that question, consider some of the techniques discussed earlier, like Object Writing, Artist's Dates or Raising Your Level of Curiosity. What is of interest to you? What would be a good message to write about? What emotion would you like to stir in your listener? What experience would you like to create?

Universal Themes

One way to approach finding subject matter is to select a universal theme and work backward. Remember, going from Personal to Universal invites inclusion and understanding. Universal themes are the abstract concepts that are important to everyone. If your specific story, idea or message can come from one of the main universal theme categories, the greater the chances people will be able to relate to it.

One commonly held view is that there are 7 universal themes:

1. Love
2. Hate
3. Loneliness
4. Happiness
5. Sadness
6. Jealousy
7. Revenge

Each theme has subsets. Love includes romantic love, love of family, friends, pets, place, the common man, and so on. Hate, Jealousy and Revenge are closely tied, and Anger would probably be a subset of all of them, but if you use these as guidelines, you probably will find a theme you can use as the umbrella for telling your story.

Another view is that there are only 2 fundamental themes that encompass all the others: Love and Fear. I find this idea quite interesting, but for practical purposes, it's too limited in number, and too broad in scope. So it's back to my list of 7 themes, or maybe a more specific list like this:

These 12 themes are the most commonly found in literature:

1. Humanity vs. Nature (sexuality, human nature, aging)
2. Humanity vs. Society (peer pressure, cultural norms)
3. Humanity's Reckoning with Divinity (destiny, free will, angry god, no god)
4. Injustice (crime doesn't pay, mistreatment)
5. Overcoming Adversity (growth through difficulty, expansion)
6. Friendship (sacrifice, fraternity)
7. Family (sacrifice, support and strength)
8. Yin and Yang (balance is always shifting and change, good or bad, is constant)
9. Love (conquers all, is the noblest of pursuits)
10. Death (is part of life, must be reckoned with)
11. Sacrifice Brings Reward (hard work and commitment pay off)
12. We're All One (despite our differences, we're all the same).

No list of universal themes is definitive, but each one offers a host of possibilities to write from. If you reflect on any one of them, you'll probably begin to see potential story lines form and ideas take shape.

Try This

1. Select a universal theme and brainstorm as many ideas as you can, related to that theme.

2. Check your existing work to see if you have a title, a first line or a draft lyric that would fit into one of the categories of universal themes. Now finish the lyric using the universal theme as a compass for decision-making.

Pre-Writing

It may be apparent by now that pre-writing, or sorting out your ideas, getting clear about the song you want to write and brokering agreement with collaborators is important to do before you begin in earnest. The following two techniques are intended for use before you start getting into the nitty-gritty of hammering out a song. They're tools for focusing on what to write about.

Before we get to these techniques, however, here is a pre-writing prerequisite: always have a recording device set up and ready to go. So many great ideas get lost in the moment. With a recorder you can retrieve those priceless ideas and keep moving forward. No time is lost trying to recreate a great idea, and as things progress, it's a working "document" you and your collaborators can reference.

Clustering

One way to trigger creativity is to use the non-linear brainstorming technique called clustering. This technique was developed for creative writing by author Gabrielle Rico, who was inspired by the right brain's ability to access wonder, chaos and a lifetime's worth of experiences. By using this technique, the "inner landscape" can be mapped and made visible, and patterns and ideas brought to the surface.

Clustering is especially good for songwriters when the goal is to develop content, but only the vaguest ideas of what to write about have surfaced. Clustering is a way to coax the left brain to be silent while using the right brain to come up with your unique thoughts and feelings on a particular subject.

Rules

This work is not necessarily meant to be shared or make sense to anyone but you (it might not make sense to you, either). Don't interrupt the clustering process until it's finished (your left brain will want to take control).

Be completely honest with whatever shows up. Write down what comes to mind, even if it makes you feel uncomfortable. Keep this work private and allow the honesty to flow. We all have our "shadow sides" – things we don't like about ourselves, but this work is intended to provide insight, and the final product can always be edited.

How to Do Clustering

1. Write the subject of your cluster (a word or a short phrase) in the middle of a clean page. Make a circle around it.

2. Look at your subject and start riffing. Let one idea lead to another and list each idea in a string. Be honest. Write down whatever comes, no matter how absurd, illogical or uncomfortable it may make you feel.

3. Eventually, your mind will draw a blank. Recognize when your ideas have dried up and stop (remember: avoid letting the left brain take over).

4. Next, have another look at the subject, and start riffing gain, letting another string of associations surface. Write them down until no more come. Do this several times until you have 3-6 strings.

5. Next, have a fresh look at each string, and write a few lyrical lines based on the string. Once you've done this for each string, see if there is a string that you could expand upon and keep going as long as things are flowing. Is there another string you could do this to? As soon as you start actively "thinking" to make new ideas come: STOP!

6. Put your cluster sheet away.

7. Come back in 5 minutes, an hour, a day, a week – but only after you've had a chance to disengage your right brain. When you come back to it, look at the entire cluster. You might be surprised by what you see. Your left brain will take over and begin organizing what it observes and making sense of what the right brain was communicating. Your right brain created a visual map of the subject from your subconscious. Can your left brain now identify a structure? Are there strings or lyrics that suggest a verse? A chorus? A main hook? Is there a logical way to organize the ideas into a coherent form for a song?

To illustrate this technique, I selected the word "homeless". The following diagram shows how I completed steps 1-4.

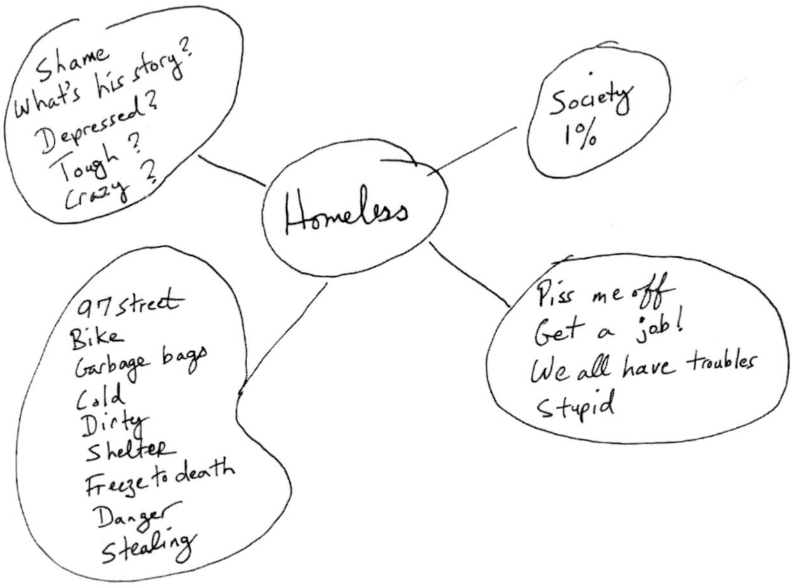

Notice how each string had a different focus (including the one that reveals my darker attitudes about homeless people). Next I stood back, had a look, and completed steps 5-7.

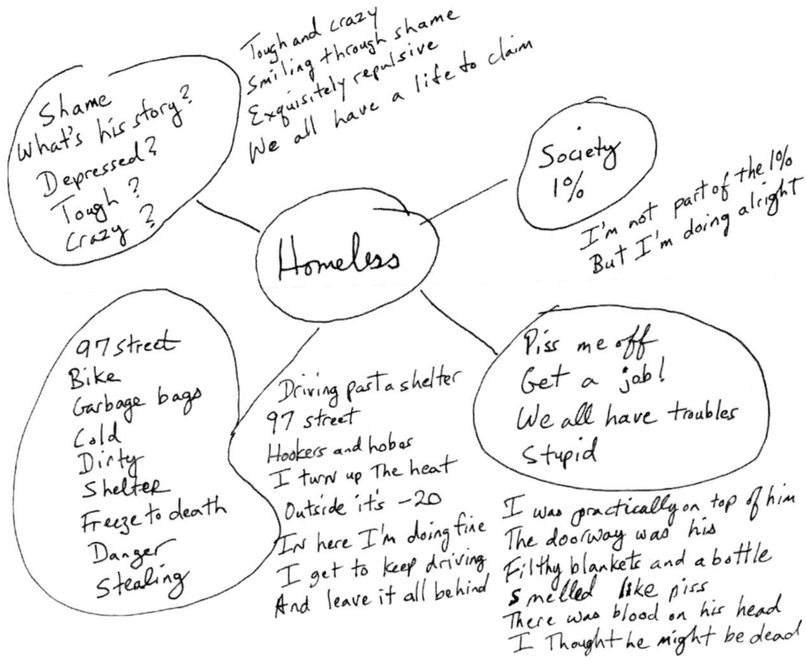

After writing some off-the cuff lyrics for each string, my left brain was later able to see a pattern emerge that suggested an order:

Verse 1:	"Practically on top of him" string. This seemed like the beginning of a story and a good place to start for verse 1.
Chorus:	"Tough and crazy" string. This felt conceptual in nature, describing the attributes of homeless people, and a good choice for a Chorus direction.

Verse 2:	"Driving past a shelter" string. This seemed very verse-like and a good follow-up to verse 1.
Bridge:	"I'm not part of the 1%" string. This seemed like it could be spun into a bridge where I could comment on my responsibility to my fellow man.

If you try this exercise, you may find it surprising (as I did) how your right brain and left brain can work together, using unfiltered creativity and intellectual acuity to crystallize ideas and set a creative path in motion.

TRY THIS

Go ahead and try clustering. If you need a word to start, try *Smirk*, *Sleepwalk* or *Betrayed*.

Song Planning

Once ideas start to form around the music, and the direction of the lyric is taking shape, it's probably time to start planning your song. I've been in writing sessions where more time was spent discussing what the song would (and would not) be about, what the progression of events should be, and what the tense, point of view and structure should be than doing the actual writing. In the end, this was time saved. Playwrights and novelists take great pains to get clear on what story they want to tell and what the sequence of events should be before they go about actually writing. Songwriters can benefit from doing this, too.

The point is not to become overly fastidious about detail, especially since you're still in the first draft phase. But making key decisions will help the process greatly by narrowing the scope and allowing you to marshal your creativity in more effective ways.

If you haven't already got to this point: Find a hook line and commit to it. If it's a musical idea, what words does it evoke? Is there a matching phrase bubbling to the surface? Once you find something that excites you, ask yourself what feelings and associations your fledgling song is suggesting. If you can find some main lyrical ideas, what lyrical key is it forming? Pull out the thesaurus and rhyming dictionary and get to work. Ask yourself: "If I were going to write a song about this, what would be the best way to tell it?" Another question you might ask: "What do I want this experience to add up to?"

From The Trenches

I once brought a song idea to a band I played in called Allez Ouest. I couldn't get these seemingly ridiculous lines out of my head: *"Oh Angélina, baby won't you put your big feet down. Oh Angélina, where you gonna lay your big feet down."* It felt catchy, though, and all four band members were singing it in no time. But it still made no sense. So we brainstormed ideas for how to make this odd lyric work, and eventually we concluded Angélina was a big-footed country girl who decides to quit working at the rodeo to go travel the world, leaving the singer heartbroken and hoping she would someday stop travelling and put her big feet back down next to him. Once we figured this out, we got the story nailed down and went about the business of writing the song.

It pays to sharpen your focus **before** you write. Here are some points to consider:

POV	I, You, He/She/They. Who is singing and to whom?
Voice	Is the Voice thinking (inner monologue): a) Alone and thinking b) With someone and thinking c) Addressing an absent person, place, thing d) Addressing the collective "You" Or in conversation with someone present?
Time Frame	When is this happening? Will this change?
Scene	What is the location? (It should at least imply where.)
Tone	What is the mood, the lyric tone?
Attitude	Are the characters educated, street-smart, poetic, cynical, naive?
Structure	What form best suits the effect you seek?

Try This

Take an idea you found in the clustering exercise and organize and plan a song using the above questions.

Check Your Work

Once you have a first draft, take a break and come back with fresh eyes to see if you've missed anything from this checklist:

- ○ The main idea is interesting.
- ○ The title is interesting.
- ○ The title appears in Spotlight Positions.
- ○ The first line is interesting.
- ○ The lines that appear in Spotlight Positions are strong.
- ○ The tone and use of language is consistent (i.e. conversational, observational, passionate).
- ○ The lyrics make sense to anyone.
- ○ The tone of the lyrics matches the music.
- ○ There are identifiable lyrical hooks.
- ○ There are identifiable musical hooks.
- ○ The melody is singable (and in a good key for the singer).
- ○ The groove is right for the song.
- ○ Each section is different and easily identified (i.e. Verse, Chorus, Bridge).
- ○ The energy flows well (melodic contours, phrasing, structure).
- ○ The lyrics flow well (each line follows the previous one logically).
- ○ The lyrics are specific, simple and action-oriented.
- ○ The (verb) tense is consistent, and any tense changes are clear.
- ○ The use of pronouns is correct.
- ○ The verses move forward (don't paraphrase each other).
- ○ The theme has universal appeal.
- ○ It's easy to answer the question "What's the song about?" in a few words.

Victoria's Secrets

Practise your Craft. Practice, practice and more practice is what develops you as a writer. Don't get stuck on re-writing the same song(s) to perfection ... just do the best you can with them in a reasonable amount of time and move on ... try new approaches and new ideas. Once you're about 1,000 songs in, you'll be getting somewhere, and your craft will be honing itself to an art.

Dare to Suck. In collaborative songwriting, that has to be your slogan. You've got to spit your ideas out into the room, no matter how dumb they might sound inside your head ... verbalize what you're thinking about as you're thinking it, instead of self-editing. It's brainstorming. There are no wrong answers – and anything that is put into the room becomes a tool that your collaborator can use to spark ideas.

Trust the Source. I don't like to consider myself the source of creative ideas – that's too much pressure to put on myself. Instead, I think of myself as the conduit to some universal source. I'm the kitchen faucet that lets the water through. I just have to open the tap and there's an endless supply of creative ideas out there for me to access. That takes the "hard" out of it – it doesn't have to be hard! Relax, and trust that the source is there for you if you just **listen** for it ... listen for the tiny melodies and quiet words in the back of your subconscious mind, and value them enough to speak them out loud and see what they might become.

Be Kind to Yourself. If you get blocked or frustrated, be aware of what your self-talk sounds like. Our inner creative beings are tender and easily bruised, like little kids. If a child were frustrated because he couldn't do something, would you tell him "You idiot! What's wrong with you! You're useless!" No? Well then, why would you speak that way to your own creative self? Instead say: "What do you need to feel better? A walk? A bath? A break? To read a book? To take a nap?" And give yourself permission to nurture yourself. That nurturing is what will draw the next song out of you much faster than beating yourself with a stick.

Co-Writing

For many years I resisted co-writing. I now wish I had started sooner. Looking back, I realize my reluctance arose from not knowing how to go about writing with another person, uncertainty around dealing with creative differences and a guarded attitude reflecting my lack of maturity as a writer.

Not everyone co-writes, and non-collaborators often cite the fact they don't feel they can achieve a satisfactory level of intimacy or authenticity by sharing songwriting duties. They feel compromise or outside influence will dilute their artistry, especially when they also wear the artist's hat. If this is you, then fair enough, keep doing what you're doing.

But if you feel co-writing is something you would like to try, there are many good reasons to start. Foremost is the fact that it'll make you grow as a writer. Our colleagues are often our best teachers, and I have learned a great deal from working with other songwriters, from emerging artists to crafty pros. It can be enlightening to see how others approach the various issues that crop up, and going through the process with another will broaden your scope as a writer. It can also be exciting to see your work take interesting turns that would not have arisen without other people bringing their talents to the table.

Another reason to co-write is that collaborations give your work more places to go. When we write with different people, it means our songs will be recorded and performed by a larger number of artists for a larger number of people. This usually results in the cultivation of a more expansive network within the industry, increased opportunity, and higher income. Again on a personal note, I have often been surprised to see, when looking at royalty statements, which songs by which artists have been receiving airplay on radio or TV, and where. You may find that a song you wrote is being played in a foreign country, or on a TV show. When you expand your circle of collaborators, you widen the net for potential exposure and revenue.

Many successful collaborations have clear-cut lines drawn around who is the composer and who is the author, making use of each partner's specific skill set. Elton John and Bernie Taupin, Burt Bacharach and Hal David, Nickolas Ashford and Valerie Simpson are examples of writing teams where duties were clearly divided (although most report feeling free to express opinions and ideas about their partner's work).

However, many collaborations involve writers who regularly create music and lyrics on their own, but enjoy working with others. Sometimes it's a desire to write with a specific person that sparks collaboration, and sometimes it's a publisher getting people together. Certain writers like the social aspect of being in a room with someone to do the work with, and sometimes it's just more fun and interesting to see what happens when creative minds collide. Co-writers can provide valuable feedback, and infuse new energy and insight to complete a song that has eluded being put to bed.

While co-writing can lead to more opportunity and increased revenue, it's also important to point out that more collaborators means smaller royalty percentages. Where a song written alone gives the writer 100% of all royalties, this percentage gets cut in half with the involvement of a co-writer, and if there are several, it will be reduced further (in most cases co-writers share equally, but more about splits later). So, on the surface, co-writing can mean less money. However, this is offset, especially over the course of a career, with the potential for gain that collaboration can bring. When we write with another, we usually end up with a finished product, and we increase the number of champions for our song. And as the old adage goes, it's better to have 50% of something than 100% of nothing.

Having additional champions for your work means having additional helpers to find homes for your songs, cover the costs of getting demos made and sent out, and sharing other tasks and responsibilities associated with songwriting, like recording, registering the songs with Performing Rights Organizations and networking. It also means you'll have someone to support you and commiserate with if your song meets with criticism or rejection.

When writing partnerships endure, relationships develop and it becomes easier to be frank and direct with each other, which invariably helps the writing process and the quality of work. Conversely, one of the most frustrating things about co-writing with a new partner can be a sense of treading on eggshells – when politesse and good manners result in the withholding of honest expression.

In order to maximize open and productive expression while also developing a new writing relationship, it's good to get clear about your goals and cover off any creative or business issues, preferably over coffee, as you're getting ready to write. This need not be a heavy discussion requiring lawyers, but a chance to line up your aspirations and ensure your time together is well spent. The range of topics to discuss may include creative direction, royalty splits, process (including follow-up rewrites), and recording of the song. It's good to have a shared understanding about anything you're not sure of before you start so that the writing relationship can begin with open communication, and there are no surprises later.

Purpose/Direction

A great starting point is to discuss the direction of the song, and if there is a particular goal for it. For instance, if you're co-writing with an artist, is there a specific type of song they're looking for? Maybe they've selected most of the songs for their next album, but are still in need of a fun, up-tempo song. Or perhaps there's a message, attitude or point of view that they want to express that hasn't been written yet. Is everything in 4/4? Do they need something in 3/4, or is there a specific groove or style that still needs to be written?

Sometimes artists are looking for several types of songs. Are there particular themes that interest them? Do these themes spark anything in you? Do you have musical or lyrical ideas to work from to get the ball rolling? It's good form to come to a writing session with an idea to present, as this can often kick-start the process. However, don't come in with ideas that you're not willing to see evolve. Clinging to your idea can be a significant roadblock in the creative process and in the development of a writing relationship. If the idea is precious to you, keep it for yourself and finish it on your own. And if your idea is headed in a direction you really don't like, diplomatically say you'd rather keep it for yourself because you have a different direction in mind, but offer an alternative if you can.

If you're writing for someone else, whether an artist or a project, make sure you're clear on what that artist or project actually need. Sometimes a 5-minute phone call can save an afternoon's worth of work.

And if you're writing for yourself, these same questions around direction and purpose can help focus your energies and ensure variety in your work.

In any case, there will be many times when you feel the tide of creativity go out on you. When this happens, have faith that there will always be a better idea coming and there's an imminent solution to any songwriting problem.

Stupid Ideas

I've heard from a few Nashville songwriters about how seasoned writers, with far more hits under their belts than the newcomers they were paired with, would set everyone at ease at a writing session by letting the other writers know they often have really stupid ideas, and they fully expect everyone else to chime in with their really stupid ideas, too. Nothing leaves the room until it's done.

These veterans know that stupid ideas lead to better ideas and help narrow down what you do want.

Creating a relaxed climate means opening the door wide for freedom of thought and risk-taking, and this usually fosters more robust exchanges. Perfectionism, especially at the "idea generation" stage, kills creativity. It can spoil the dynamic when, for instance, two writers engage in the spirit of "there are no stupid ideas," and a third party is quietly working away, but never communicating their thoughts until they feel safe to do so. This is counter-productive, and is usually a result of insecurity or perfectionism. We all tend to suffer from these tendencies to some degree, but if you're not willing to step past them, then co-writing may prove particularly difficult.

The freedom to offer stupid ideas should also come with the ability to let go when they get tossed out. By not taking the rejection of ideas personally, it sends a message that you believe in yourself (there will always be more ideas), and that you won't judge others when their ideas get rejected. Another way to frame this is to adopt the mantra that "the best idea wins." This attitude can also set the foundation that will allow you to stand up for an idea you believe didn't get its fair shake and is worth re-visiting.

I've seen this happen over and over again at writing sessions. Sometimes we get lost in our writing bubble, and fail to fully grasp an idea that has merit. Sometimes you need to let a little time pass and restate the idea, at least until you know it has been fully heard. But you can't win 'em all, so if it ultimately gets rejected, move on. And once in a while, ideas get resurrected a few hours down the road.

Splits

For most songs, the share of royalties is split evenly among all the people who have come together to write the song. Although this is usually an unstated agreement, it can be good to make sure everyone is on board before the work begins. I know of cases where a (usually novice) songwriter will examine the final product, break down who wrote what, and make an argument for a redistribution of royalties based on lines written or musical ideas accepted. Besides the fact this approach won't attract a lot of second-time collaborators, it reveals a short-sighted view of the process.

It happens often that an idea one person came up with sets the ball in motion, but along the way this idea disappears or is transformed. When tracing the evolution of the song, however, the idea was pivotal to the process, and the song would probably not exist in its finished form without this catalyst. The same can be said about every idea that appeared along the way – the ones that lead to other ones, or the abandoned ideas that helped solidify what the song needed by clarifying the parameters.

While it's true it can feel unfair to credit everyone equally when the real work is carried out by one or two people, the argument can be made that the ideas the less involved person contributed helped form the final product, and are worthy of equal share. This is particularly true when there is a working relationship already established among mature songwriters.

From The Trenches

In the band Allez Ouest, all four band members got together to write songs for an album. Because we knew each other well, we were comfortable in asserting ourselves in the throes of creativity, and in sitting back and listening actively and lending energy and enthusiasm when we weren't the ones coming up with the ideas. As a result, I can point out who wrote much of each song, but I feel that every song, even the ones I had the biggest hand in writing, are 100% band collaborations that benefited from the input, both passive and active, of each member.

For bands looking to write together, be aware that songs are generally defined as melody and lyrics, so there are important discussions to have about royalty splits before you write. Coming to a solid agreement can allow creativity to flow, and this is particularly important for bands that jam together to create songs.

In most cases, there are one or two predominant songwriters who bring songs to the band or hunker down to put melody and lyrics to a song the band was jamming on. Sometimes these songwriters choose to share a portion of royalties with other band members to foster a positive environment, and recognize their contributions by spreading the wealth around. This is a double-edged sword, however. If royalties are not shared, resentment can build when non-writing band members realize they are not able to capitalize on a revenue stream that others in the band are receiving. But acrimony can also develop when a songwriter puts in a significant number of extra hours creating and refining the songs that the future of the band will live and die on, and royalty sharing feels unjust. Finding the balance can be tricky and requires honest communication. Some bands split everything evenly and credit all band members, while others give majority shares to the principal writers (who retain full credit) and smaller percentages to the non-writing musicians (who do not receive credit). And many do no royalty sharing at all, attributing royalties and credits on a song per song basis.

For songwriters who do share royalties with band members, royalty splits can have time limits (i.e for the duration of the band or while a player is an active member, plus three years), after which they revert to the writers. Each group needs to evaluate their specific situation to arrive at the best scenario. A key question for songwriters is how important the band is to the success of the song - are the players core members of a group or hired guns? There will be other industry players, such as publishers, producers and managers who may also want a piece of the pie, so don't be too eager to give your intellectual property rights away in the interests of being nice. Do so because it makes good business sense.

There are special circumstances, where it is appropriate for certain writers to receive less than others in the split. Sometimes people get invited into the process after a song has been crafted, but still needs refinement. For instance, there have been a few times where I contributed a bridge to a song I was producing, and I felt it appropriate to take a smaller percentage than what the main writers were getting. I suppose I could have also made the argument that my contribution was of equal value because the song wouldn't have been finished otherwise, but I preferred maintaining good relationships to squeezing out a few more points. However, any time a writer gets parachuted into the creative process, they deserve to receive a share of the royalties. How much is up for negotiation.

And then there are translations. If you've ever translated a song into another language, you know that literal translations almost never work. Some songs can stay close to the original lyric, but at the extreme, some translations are complete reinventions of the original lyric, and require a great deal of work. I know an artist who translated a Gordon Lightfoot song into French for an album he did. It took years to get permission and final approval, and in the end, my friend received zero royalties. However, in most cases (in Canada), the translator is entitled to up 50% of the portion of royalties allotted for lyrics. This, too, should be discussed if it feels relevant. In situations where I've done commissioned work, I've stipulated that any translations into French require my approval.

If anyone in the room is signed to a publishing deal, there needs to be some agreement about how the publishing splits will go. Most publishers routinely do co-publishing deals, but once in a while songwriters signed to a company are forbidden to co-write with writers not signed to the same company. If you are an unpublished writer, working with a signed writer can be a good way to make connections and find a way in to a publisher.

Similarly, some discussion is needed about demoing the song, preferably before the song is written. A basic voice/instrument recording can be done without any big cash outlay. But, if the song is going to be pitched to industry players, it needs to be professionally recorded, and that could mean hiring producers, musicians and singers. Sometimes one of the writers is in a position to do this, and various deals can be struck to make it happen ("spec" deals, for example, where the producer gets paid if the song gets cut; or the first royalties received get paid back to the producer until he has recouped his investment).

Exploitation

Exploitation sounds like such a bad word, but when it comes to songwriting, it's actually a good thing. The way songs generally make money is when they're exploited, or in other words, used for commercial gain – in films, on radio, on TV, etc. When a song gets exploited, it can show up in a variety of places, and this is where songwriters derive their income – from performance, mechanical and other royalties.

When you collaborate on a song for an artist, sometimes an assumption is made that the artist will get first crack at recording the song. This might be an unspoken understanding, but it would be good to discuss it anyway. What if a year or two goes by and that artist never releases it? Shouldn't you be allowed to try to interest other artists in the song? This is your work, too, and being nice isn't helping put food on the table. In such cases, it would likely be fair to give the artist a year to record the song before you try to drum up interest from others, but a larger discussion about exploitation should probably occur at the outset.

From The Trenches

Once again, I learned this from personal experience. Years ago I co-wrote the music for a musical with a very talented singer-songwriter. Unfortunately, she decided shortly after she no longer wanted to be in show business. While I found this a shame (thankfully she later returned to show biz and has had a great career), it was also frustrating because she wouldn't let anyone else record the songs we had written until she did. One of these songs had garnered interest from a famous Canadian singer, and we never capitalized on it. In these situations, the artist sometimes needs to be reminded that the work belongs to both of you, and you should always be allowed to find a home for your songs.

Over time, this artist realized it was to her benefit to have her work exploited, whether by her or someone else, and we went on to write many more songs and signed publishing deals for our work. Similarly, lots of artists, aware of the merits of having other people sing their songs, also write songs for other artists (Dolly Parton, Meghan Trainor, Prince), for the joy of having their work get out into the world, the fun of hearing it performed by others, and for the extra source of income.

In his book *The Songwriter's Guide to Collaboration,* Walter Carter refers to several kinds of writers and the roles they assume within a partnership. Sometimes established writers are more valuable for the connections they offer than for their writing abilities; newcomers can inject enthusiasm and energy. Some of us are Idea People, whose great ideas get things started. Cleanup writers (or Closers) are really good at seeing what a song needs and polishing it off. Others, especially instrumentalists, are riff, hook and groove specialists. And Song Doctors are able to bring a song back from the brink by examining its problems and fixing them.

Sometimes you're the Closer in one partnership and the Ideas Person in the next, or even from song to song, and acquiring all these skills and aptitudes makes for a well-rounded songwriter.

Are We Done Yet?

Rewriting is part of songwriting, and this is as true of collaborations as it is of solo writing. Sometimes at the end of a session, it's clear that more work needs to be done and a follow-up date is arranged to re-examine the song and finish it off with a clear perspective and fresh energy. And sometimes it takes a little distance and time away from a song to notice the problem spots, and it's a good idea to give the song a few days or even weeks away in order to evaluate what you've created.

With some songs, the rewrites are minimal and can be accomplished by a few rounds of email exchanges that everyone signs off on. But if these fixes start creating other problems, then it's probably time to get back together in the same room.

An important point to remember is that any work started together should generally be finished together. It's not acceptable for one writer to bring a song in to work on, spend a few hours in collaboration, and then take it away to finish on their own (or worse, bring it to someone else). Follow-up sessions should be organized to complete the song together (and new ideas can be brought forward at this time). As mentioned above, if you have reservations about the direction a writing session is taking on a song you brought in, then stop working on it as soon as possible, and politely and professionally make it clear you don't intend to keep any of the new ideas, and move on (with enthusiasm) to another song.

When working in pairs or groups, it can be hard to resist the urge to declare that the song is ready when it isn't. There is a wonderful optimism that a group can provide, and it can be daunting to crush this enthusiasm by being a stickler for detail and pointing out flaws long past the point when people want to keep working on the song. Fatigue can be a major factor in these situations. Remember we all have different biorhythms and work capacities; short but frequent breaks can really help. When the partnership has hit a wall, and you feel others are saying the song is good when it's really only good enough, it's time to take a break or schedule a follow-up session.

There may have been a way, however, to prevent getting to this point. If you pay attention, you can probably sense when there is a drop in energy and ideas become almost impossible to coax out. When this happens, stand up, do something else for a few minutes and disengage. In a group, there can be pressure to keep the collective nose to the grindstone. Beware of this notion and reject it. If you need to take a break, then do it. There's a good chance your partner(s) will be relieved you did and see this as permission to do likewise. In the end, taking breaks can prevent fatigue from setting in and bad choices being made, leading to higher productivity, better results and more fun.

Credit Where Credit Is Due

One aspect of songwriting that can be hard on the ego is when an artist receives all the accolades for a song and little or no credit is given to the writers. While much of this comes with the territory, artists should be aware that other careers are tied up in their songs, from songwriters and publishers to producers, arrangers, musicians, publicists, agents, managers and parents(!). Giving credit to these people goes a long way in developing industry support and makes the artist look like a class act. The flipside is that songwriters also need to accept the fact that their work often goes unheralded, and there needs to be intrinsic satisfaction derived from doing good work.

Try This

1. ***Find a writing partner and select a theme to write about.*** Try using the techniques discussed on Clustering and Song Planning in chapter 10, "Process".

2. ***If you are writing for a specific artist (either to pitch them a song, or to try and write your own version of a song that inspired you), analyze their work, or a specific song and discuss which elements contributed most towards its success.*** This will help you understand how to approach the task, and assist in spotting any places where you may be too close to plagiarizing instead of creating music "inspired by"...

Being Your Own Producer

Once upon a time, songwriters and artists were rarely the same people, and the music industry only required songwriters to be able to write songs. The pitching was done by song pluggers, who performed the latest creations in an office for the stars of day, or in a store for the public. The main goal was to have your songs performed so sheet music could be sold. But times changed.

As radio and television developed, the recording industry also grew in prominence, and the end game shifted from selling sheet music to monetizing songs through radio airplay and record sales. Artists saw songwriting as a new and important revenue stream, and wanted in on the action. As the industry grew, artists signed development deals, working on new material until it was ready for release, and demos were recorded by the labels on an ongoing basis. Publishers also recorded demos so they could interest artists in their writers' songs, or pitch a band or artist to a label to get signed. And for any artist or band wanting to get signed to a label or a publisher (or even get gigs), having a high quality demo was essential. But times changed again.

As record sales dwindled in recent years, budgets for demos have all but evaporated, and the number of artists requiring demos has decreased even further (in certain fields like Rock and Hip Hop, artists overwhelmingly write their own material). Some publishers and record labels still pay for demos to be made, especially in Country music, but where demo sessions used to require a producer and a handful of musicians, publishers now give their signed writers a fraction of what they used to get to record demos, and are usually expected to do it themselves.

Where does that leave the songwriter? If you're a solo artist or part of a band, there's a good chance you'll be expected to create high quality recordings if you want to get signed, but in most cases, a record deal proves elusive, and these recordings become independent commercial releases. These days the word "demo" is heard less and less.

For songwriters who don't intend to also be artists, you'll need to get your recordings to a level where you feel comfortable handing them or uploading them to people in the business.

If you're saying to yourself that this seems grossly unfair, I hear you. So take some time to wallow in the injustice. When you're ready to move on, try to look at this as another skill set you can develop that will make your work better, and will give you freedom and independence. In today's music, production has all but replaced traditional arranging, and the more you understand how to work the gears, the better it will be for your music, your control over it and your appreciation for all aspects of song development.

Goals and Expectations

For some, the studio serves as an important sketchpad, and replaces traditional instruments as a tool for writing. For others, it's a means for capturing and recording finished work and making it accessible.

If the role of producer is new for you, I'd suggest setting the following goal as your first target:

> To make recordings that can be presented to industry people (artists, publishers, music directors) without apology.

From there, your next goal should be:

> To make recordings that are ready for commercial release.

What does all this mean? It's beyond the scope of this book to provide a detailed manual on recording. There are lots of terrific courses and online instructionals for that. Instead, I'd like to give an overview to get you started.

In Tune, In Time

Musically, performances need to be in tune and in time. This requires capturing performances that are professional enough to have industry people take the work seriously. For all performers, this means having excellent rhythm. To maintain a sense of time as strong as it can be, most recordings are done to a click track, so learn how to use one and make sure your performers are able to play/sing to it.

Most recordings are also done to a grid to maximize rhythmic synchronization. A grid syncs perfectly with the tempo of the song (which you specify), and enables audio to be moved and lined up with the grid where fixes are necessary, and for midi instruments to be quantized digitally to match the grid. The grid also allows you to create a tempo map to accommodate such intentional time fluctuations as ritardando and accelerando.

As for tuning, it's always best to hire musicians who are of high calibre and whose sense of pitch is strong. This being said, there may be times when you want to correct the pitch of a note or a phrase that was sung or played. This decision is a personal and often philosophical one, and I'm not going to posit a moral argument either way. Suffice to say that most songs on the radio have been pitch-corrected. If this is something you want to do, make sure you learn how to do it properly (you need to be actively involved). When auto-tune is done badly, it sounds terrible, and I'm aware of more than one case where the pitch was "corrected" to the wrong note.

Essential Gear

There are many affordable digital audio work stations (DAWs) on the market today, and for less than what it used to cost to record one song, you can get set up with a fully functional recording rig.

What you will need is a computer, an interface that goes between the computer and your instrument/microphone, a condenser mic and some decent headphones and monitors.

The computer needs to have sufficient power and memory to run whatever DAW you purchase. Most of my students use Macs for music, and Macs are equipped with Garageband, an excellent, free program that comes with a wide variety of plugins. Prices vary on other programs, like Protools and Logic, which offer more features. Whatever DAW you pick, you will need an interface you can use to plug in instruments, vocals and midi instruments. They usually have a headphone jack and a +48V switch for phantom power (to use with condenser microphones). The smaller interfaces have only two inputs that can be used for either XLR or ¼ inch cables. Larger interfaces come in racks and have more inputs (necessary only if you are recording many instruments, like drums, at the same time).

Assuming you already have instruments to record with, the next step is getting at least one professional microphone. Do not use a dynamic microphone, like a Shure SM58 to record with. These are excellent live mics, but not the right tool for recording. If you can only afford one mic, make sure it is a condenser mic (with a large diaphragm with a diameter of one inch or more). The great ones will cost several thousand dollars, but entry-level pro condenser mics can cost as little as a few hundred bucks. You can use them on everything. Remember, these mics also require phantom power.

If you have a little more cash, it can be great to have a matched pair of small diaphragm ("pencil") condenser mics as well (with a diameter of one inch or less), especially for stereo mic'ing (i.e. acoustic guitars).

In broad terms, large condenser mics are more sensitive and have more bass response, which make them excellent for vocals and room mic'ing. Small condenser mics tend to be a little quieter and have less low end, and work well with most acoustic instruments and as overhead mics for drums and percussion. The only time you might consider using a dynamic mic is when mic'ing guitar amps and snare drums. For these applications, the Shure SM57 has long been a workhorse.

For headphones, you'll need to invest in a decent pair (usually a few hundred bucks) if you want to mix on them. You'll also need to buy some pro monitors for mixing. Talk to the folks who sell this gear and ask about the best options. There is no point investing in recording gear if you can't trust what you're hearing, especially if you're trying to record with entry-level equipment. So spend the money on your monitors, and be sure to treat the room for any acoustic issues like standing waves and bass traps in both the recording and mixing environments (sorry, you're going to have to read a few articles about this or buy a sound engineer a case of beer to check out your place).

One more essential – you'll need a "popper-stopper" for the vocal mic. These are small screens that minimize the effect of "pops and clicks" produced by the voice (especially by the sounds of P, B and K) and can be purchased at most music stores. They can also be made by stretching out a coat hanger and placing panty-hose over it (and duct-taping it to a mic stand).

Finally, a piece of gear that is not essential, but tops the "good to have" list is the mic preamp. A good mic preamp can add warmth and musicality to the sound, particularly if it has tube circuitry, and the high end ones make an appreciable difference to the sound quality.

A Few Basic Recording Tips

Certain singers put out a lot of sound pressure, and this can beat up the capsule of your microphone and create distortion. Make sure singers are at least 4 to 6 inches away from the mic – or more according to the level of sound pressure they're putting out. This will also minimize any "proximity effect" – the rumble, runaway plosives and general ugliness that occurs when the singer is too close to the mic. If your mic is still being overwhelmed by a powerful singer or a loud guitar amp, there may be a switch on the mic called a pad that will reduce the mic's output. Use it and then turn up the input a little as needed.

If your mic or your interface has a low cut filter (also known as a high pass filter), it's a good thing to use most of the time. It will help clean up much of the unwanted low end that can muddy a mix and create noise. For things like acoustic guitars and voices, there is usually very little information in that range, anyway.

When mic'ing an acoustic guitar, most people place the mic a few inches from the 12th fret. This seems to be a good sonic compromise between the scratchy high end of the neck and the boomy thud of the low end. When stereo mic'ing an acoustic, there are several techniques you could use (the main concern is to avoid creating phasing problems caused by poor mic placement), but one of the most popular is to aim one mic a little above the 12th fret and the other toward the bridge of the instrument. Blend the two to taste.

Many excellent drum and percussion programs offer the options of using pre-recorded parts or creating your own with Midi. The pre-recorded parts can be altered if you use Grid and Midi, so if a bass drum is not where you want it, for instance, you can move it, delete it or add more. When creating drum tracks, it helps to have an understanding of how to play drums so the parts sound natural (try taking a lesson or two if this is foreign to you).

Signals that get recorded should never hit the red zone on the fader, as they probably will sound distorted (and be unusable) in the mix. In general, signals should fall somewhere between -17 and 0 on the fader when being recorded. Anything below that may also cause problems because of weak signal and associated noise.

The Recording Process

In the same way that songwriters are now expected to be producers, producers are now expected to be engineers. And everyone has to be a business person, time manager and strategic planner, too. But if you have taken on the challenges of self-producing, then you've also developed your engineering skills. And if you've got your songs to a place where they're airtight in terms of music, lyrics, arrangement, key, etc., then you've also succeeded in tackling the quality control aspect of producing. You've maximized your chances of success and are ready to apply for your official producer button. So let's go!

There are 6 basic steps to producing a song (or album).

1. Pre-Production

This is the work of writing and refining the songs, picking the best ones, developing killer arrangements, selecting keys and tempos, and hiring the best people. This may also be the time to refine your vision, image and conceptual ideas, and make sure they line up with all the musical elements. Unfortunately, this is the part of the process that gets the least amount of attention, when it should get the most.

2. Bed Tracks

Whether the tracks are recorded by human beings or by samples and keyboards, most recordings start with rhythm tracks (usually bass and drums), and at least one chord instrument to provide the key and help make sense of the arrangement (a "scratch" vocal track is often recorded at this time as well as a reference). These foundational tracks are called the bed tracks, and they are used to layer other tracks onto. If these tracks feel good, then your finished song stands a great chance of sounding good, too. But if they don't, it's hard to create a great sounding song with a shaky foundation. Get the best players you can.

If you're recording a drum kit, (and you have the budget), you might want to go to a pro recording studio to capture well-recorded sounds. However, a project studio or well-treated room in the home can work well with a little love and attention to detail.

3. Overdubs

Once the bed tracks have been recorded, overdubs can begin. These tracks are usually recorded one person at a time. Recording them away from a commercial studio can still yield good results if you're careful, with the added bonus of not being on the clock. Typical overdubs include guitars, keyboards, vocals, percussion, saxophones, trumpets, violins, etc.

4. Editing

Once overdubs are complete, the editing can begin. These are the unseen hours producers put in, compiling vocal and other tracks (this involves auditioning different performances of the same instrument or voice recorded on virtual tracks and selecting the best takes until the track is compiled), pitch correcting, moving notes to make them more rhythmically accurate, eliminating or minimizing squeaks, pops, clicks, lip smacks and other noises.

5. Mixing

Mixing refers to the process of balancing all the recorded tracks and using various processors and other plugins to create ambience, colour and impact. Below is a brief description of the various mixing tools and processes.

Reverb is an important effect that can create ambience and add depth to your mix. The type of reverb you might use on a snare drum will probably differ from the vocal reverb in length and number of reflections. If your DAW allows for it, learn how to set up reverb buses and route each channel using reverb to its appropriate bus.

Delay is another great effect that can create mood and colour. It is used most often on vocals and guitars, with various types of delay – from slapback (quick delay that almost creates a doubling effect), to long delays that create a spacey effect.

Other commonly used effects are flange, chorus, distortion and wah. As with reverb, get used to creating separate buses for these effects and routing channels to them.

Panning involves placing instruments in specific locations across the aural spectrum to create interest and add depth. In most cases, the lead vocal, bass, bass drum and snare drum get panned in the centre, but all other instruments can be panned to various locations from left to right. One main goal is to keep the vocal from being crowded by having instruments too close to it, so try to find a balance for the instruments that gives each its own place in the mix, yet allows the vocal to be heard.

Equalization can add clarity to your mix. A common problem for mixes is a buildup of information, often within the midrange frequencies. By getting rid of some of these frequencies, instrument by instrument, you can open up the sound of the mix. A useful technique is to isolate an instrument or voice by soloing it, and then picking a frequency and boosting it in an exaggerated manner. Sweep to the left and right until you discover which precise frequencies build up the most. Now see what happens if you cut them. Use the "Q" to affect the bandwidth and make the size of these cuts smaller or bigger, and take small steps. Drastic cuts usually mean the instrument was poorly recorded in the first place. It's not uncommon for an EQ to have several sound alterations (for instance, roll off the low end below 64hz, make a small cut around 400hz, and boost above 6Khz). EQ's allow you to switch between different settings, with the two most commonly used being "notch" and "shelf". Most EQ's default to the notch position (and is the setting to be used for the above use of Q), which allows you to focus on specific isolated frequencies to either cut or boost. By switching to shelf, however, you can set a frequency as the point after which only higher frequencies can get through (this is called "high pass filter" and is effective for reducing rumble). You can do a similar thing at the other end of the spectrum (set a point where only frequencies below may pass), or use it to boost high-end frequencies to add clarity and presence. When the sonics of each instrument are cleaned up, the mix will sound clearer and have more impact. EQ'ing can also be used on the overall mix.

Compression is useful tool for controlling dynamics and adding impact. Compressors can be particularly tricky, however, so be cautious until you know what you're doing. Their main function is to rein in a sound source that has a wide dynamic range for the sound to sit better in the mix (with fewer peaks to manage and a more consistent output level). The main controls are Threshold, Attack, Release, Ratio and Gain. Threshold is set at the point when you want the compression to start doing its work. The Attack determines how quickly it works, and the Release determines how soon the compression lets go of the signal. The Ratio setting is used to indicate how much compression gets applied to the signal. The higher the ratio, the more compression is being used. Finally, Gain can be used to make up some of the attenuation lost when compression squashes a signal. Compression does a great job in evening out a sound, but overuse can make things sound unnatural and cause the oddly undulating effect of pumping (where you hear the compressor working hard, and its attack and release points don't jive with the rhythm of the song). And while compressors compress the signal to make it more manageable, bringing the overall level down, it will also bring up the sound floor – hiss, amp noise and other background noises. On professional mixes, most tracks receive some degree of compression, and compression is once again used for Mastering.

Volume is another feature of mixing that must be managed. With the advent of DAWs, what used to require all hands on deck, can now be done with the click of a mouse. When doing a mix, each instrument may need some adjustments to volume, and this can be automated on most DAWs. For instance, vocals usually need the most attention to volume, and care is taken to make sure the levels are consistent throughout the song, and certain phrases or syllables may be boosted or "ducked" to make them fit with the track. DAWs will allow you to automate any moves you make with the faders, or simply use a tool to write the volume changes onto a graph.

Automation can also be used for other key functions, including muting, panning and managing plugins (turning them on and off, automating changes in volume and EQ, etc.).

6. Mastering

For many of us, Mastering feels a little like alchemy. I usually leave it to the pros who do it on a daily basis and know what will work in the industry and on radio. However, for demos and other projects that need a little mastering, but aren't being commercially released, I often do my own mastering, using one of the many plugins available.

Mastering is the final stage in the preparation of audio for market. One of its prime functions is to make the music competitively loud. Mastering came about decades ago when engineers realized they could raise the overall volume of a song if they ran it through a compressor, reduced the dynamic range and turned the overall volume up. This resulted in their songs sounding louder on radio than the song before it, and "mastering wars" began. Many people feel mastering has been taken to an extreme, with dynamic range and musicality being regularly compromised to make the volume as loud as possible. Nowadays, there is a movement back to more reasonable mastering levels in the interests of making the music sound better.

Mastering is also the final step where EQ can be tweaked. With relatively sophisticated mastering gear, engineers can, for instance, fatten up the low end and brighten up the highs, or correct general frequency issues while also raising the overall level.

Finally, a mastering engineer will put everything together so the manufacturer can reproduce the music, by placing the songs in order, adjusting the time between songs and refining fades and embedding UPC or ISRC codes that allow your music to be tracked (by Nielsen Soundscan) for payment by performing rights societies.

Business

The business side of songwriting has become unrecognisable from the days publishing was concerned solely with the sale of sheet music. After the 50-year blip where record, cassette and CD sales made multimillionaires out of many fortunate musicians, it appears that the internet has doused the fire that drove the record industry. A less heady balance is being struck between the sale of recorded music and the commercialization of live performance for working musicians.

Shifts in the business of music are occurring all the time, and it's proving very difficult to stay abreast of the vagaries of the music industry's ever-changing landscape. In the hopes of providing some solid footing, let's look at traditional models of monetization and some prominent developments in the industry, while bearing in mind that the business is always evolving, and transitions and innovations can result in both challenges and opportunities.

I should point out that the rights and organizations discussed here are all Canadian, but similar ones exist in most other countries. In 1961, Canada signed the *Rome Convention for the Protection of Performers, Producers of Phonograms and Broadcasting Organizations*. This international treaty means countries allow reciprocal treatment to rights holders of participating countries. As a signatory to the Rome Convention, Canada agrees to pay foreign rights holders whose sound recordings are broadcast or performed in this country and vice-versa. Fifty-eight countries signed the Rome Convention, including the U.K, Germany, France, Italy, Spain, Australia and Japan. Notably absent is the U.S.A, but Canada has reciprocal agreements with our southern neighbour independent of the Rome Convention.

As the sale of music has declined exponentially, many artists have staked a new claim: since recorded music can no longer be relied upon as a major source of revenue, it might as well be given away as a means of promotion and as a branding tool. This has resulted in the further devaluation of music as a commodity, and placed artists in greater financial straits than ever – the chances of making a return on investment for an album is now highly improbable for most artists. A few decades ago, people used to buy albums, bring them home and actively listen to them. Now they are accustomed to paying next to nothing for the music they consume, and most often do their listening in unfocused environments (i.e. while driving or working out). For these reasons, most artists see the most viable way to make money on recorded music is to sell it at live shows.

Performers and songwriters make money in very different ways. Artists, bandmates and sidemen all earn a performance fee for work done at a gig, or for services rendered in the recording studio, on television, in a film/video, etc. Additional money might be made from the sale of such products as CDs, T-shirts, books, photos, fridge magnets, spirits, condoms, etc., at a live gig or on the Internet (including iTunes and other digital distribution services.). But as a performer, the predominant means of making money are fees for service and product sales.

Now let's look at the various ways income can be derived from the intellectual property of songwriting.

Legal Considerations

First off, as soon as you write a song, you own the copyright. There is nothing you have to do to obtain it – you (and your co-writers) possess copyright by virtue of creation. However, there may be a need to protect it. For this reason, it's wise to create a recording with clear lyrics, and/or write out the lyrics and the music. This is referred to as "fixing" the work into a written or recorded form for documentation purposes.

If you ever need to legally pursue someone you feel has stolen your work, or if you ever need to defend yourself from accusations of copyright infringement, it is crucial that you can prove you owned the fixed work before the other party did.

The Songwriters Association of Canada (SAC) advises: "The Register of Copyrights in Ottawa will register a title only and your claim to ownership for a substantial fee, and such a registration is recommended if you anticipate any formal legal action on a specific title." The United States Copyright Office is another place that people from all over the world register their copyrights. Copyright lasts for the life of the creator plus 50 years, or 70 years since publication (life plus 70 years in the U.S), after which it enters the public domain.

As the SAC notes, it's expensive to do this. As an alternative, they have developed the Canadian Song Vault: "Songwriters (Association of Canada) has obtained the services of Recall, a professional information management firm operating in 17 countries across 5 continents. At Recall's highly secure Canadian information centre, your song deposits on audio CD/cassette are filed with a barcode tracking system and kept safe from dust, light, smoke and other harmful impurities to preserve their longevity."

The song vault is a cheaper option, but still costs the songwriter to register – and this fee can add up with a large catalogue. However, songs are housed indefinitely. If your membership lapses, songs remain protected, but you will need to reinstate yourself as a member if you need to use the service.

As a third option, Bemuso (a U.K resource for independent artists, DIY record labels and self-publishers) offers this: "By far the best way to establish your use and the existence of a work is to make it commercially available under your name." In other words, once you have released your music to the world commercially, you should be able to prove its existence from that date forward.

Publishing

It is important to note that copyright can be assigned to others, as happens when you agree to allow a publisher to exploit your work. Songs are generally divided into two equal parts – 50% songwriting and 50% publishing. Until you assign the publishing rights to someone else, the songwriter(s) automatically owns both the songwriting and publishing rights. In Canada, no publisher is legally allowed to take more than 50% of the song. However, songwriters may negotiate deals whereby they retain a portion of the publishing (especially if they have their own publishing company).

So, until publishing rights are assigned elsewhere, the songwriter retains 100% of the song. When working with co-writers, it's important to determine the percentage splits that each writer will receive (**see Chapter 11, Co-Writing for more on this**) and declare these splits with the Society of Composers, Authors and Music Publishers of Canada (more on SOCAN below).

If you choose to assign your publishing rights to another party, they typically receive 50% of the song, and as the creator, you retain the other 50%. This means co-writers draw from the portion attributed to songwriting only, significantly reducing the percentage they can generate income from.

For instance, before signing with a publisher, 2 co-writers own 50% of the entire song. Once a publishing agreement has been signed, the 2 co-writers now own only 50% each of the 50% they retain for songwriting. Essentially, each person's royalty has been cut in half (they each now own 25% of the entire song). Naturally, this split dwindles further when there are 3 co-writers, who go from sharing $\frac{1}{3}^{\text{rd}}$ each of the entire song to only $\frac{1}{6}^{\text{th}}$ when publishing rights are signed away.

So why sign with a publisher? The best reason is you believe they can get your music into the hands of people who can make money with it. A publisher should have access to artists, music directors, advertisers and other industry people who can exploit your song and generate revenue from it. They should be able to monetize your work by getting it to people and creating opportunities you couldn't otherwise, and free your time so you can focus on writing music. A word of caution, though: don't sign with publishers who don't deal with your kind of music – they probably won't be able to help you much.

Publishers might also be able to provide an advance against royalties, providing an income for the songwriter. The publisher usually recoups the advance before the writer can start earning royalties from the song, but in most cases, these advances don't need to be paid back even if the song earns less than the advance.

In the past, most songs were signed over to a publisher for life, but nowadays there is much more room for negotiation. It's now common for an agreement to last 3 to 5 years, with an option to renew. This gives writers a chance to take their song elsewhere if nothing has happened within the term, or re-commit to another term if they feel the company still supports the song.

Other parties who might want a piece of your royalty include producers, artists, managers and bandmates. Don't hand away royalties if you don't need to, and get signed agreements if you do. For instance, if managers want a piece of the action, ask them to commit to specific goals they will achieve to merit a percentage, and tie payouts to performance. If it's a condition of working with big-time producers, then try to establish a finite term or a maximum payout after which they are no longer eligible to receive royalties. And if an artist wants a percentage for merely recording your song, decide whether the potential for success outweighs the feeling of injustice you might feel (you might be able to get over this quickly once big royalty cheques start rolling in).

Few publishers take unsolicited material. However, you can meet them at industry events, and respectfully ask if you can send them material. If they say yes, try to get a business card as this will give you contact information and provide proof to a protective secretary that you actually met and were given the green light (some people even tape the card to the submission package or send a photo of it in an email). Resist the temptation to send everything you've ever written. Keep it to 1 to 3 of your very best songs, and make sure they're songs the publisher can actually do something with (i.e. don't send Country tunes to a Rap publisher). Another good way to meet publishers is to co-write with a staff songwriter or a signed artist (**See Chapter 11, Co-Writing**).

Ethical Considerations

There will be times when you need to balance the potential for opportunity with a perception of personal exploitation – when somebody wants a percentage of your work for no real contribution. You might also feel this way if you sign with a publisher, but do all the legwork to get your song placed with a major artist (although this does happen innocently enough from time to time).

Sometimes you have to decide whether a disagreeable situation is the "cost of doing business" or something to walk away from. I can tell you that my tendency has been to walk away, but I understand why others would choose a different path.

A friend of mine did some ghost-writing for a well-known film composer in L.A. He was paid handsomely for his work, which went a long way toward supporting his family. However, the deal required my friend to relinquish all rights to the work he had supplied (for a famous movie), and to transfer all written credit to the composer, who was already being paid a sizable fee for "writing" the music and was going to further receive royalties and recognition for the music he didn't create. The last time my friend worked for this composer, he was invited to hang out and go for a ride to a local car dealership. The purpose of the mission was to help the composer decide the colour of the new high-end sports car he was going to buy, as he'd grown tired of the old one.

I'm sorry to say that ghost-writing is common in the film industry these days. Many find this practise immoral and unethical as it exploits musicians who are eager to break into the business but need to earn a living. Another common practise is for production companies to pay composers and songwriters a flat fee for their work, but require a transfer of 100% copyright ownership to the company. The composer receives a fee for service, but no control over the work beyond that and no chance for royalties. Therefore, if a song from the soundtrack were to become a hit, the production company would reap the rewards, and the composer would receive no royalties of any kind.

While I find the more egregious actions here to be those of the industry people, I also feel that musicians have some responsibility to not undercut each other, or enter into agreements that will make it hard for others to follow in their footsteps or cause business conditions to deteriorate. Unfortunately, sharks in the industry know just how hard that is, and have no trouble finding composers and songwriters to take advantage of.

Record Deals

Record deals are similar to publishing deals in that the best reason to sign one is the label should be able to do much more for you than you can on your own. It's not unusual to sign a record deal with one company and have a publishing deal with another, and the songwriters earn royalties from the publishing deals they sign in addition to a percentage of music sales payable to them by the label as an artist. This percentage of sales can be very small, and artists need to do the math to determine whether it makes sense to sign with a label.

A label can serve many functions. A prime function is to fund the recording of albums, usually 3 to 5 over 3 to 7 years. A band may receive upwards of $30,000 to record an album, but, unless you have a great lawyer or a prominent profile, this money must be repaid through album sales, and with the advent of all-inclusive "360" deals (where artists must share revenue streams from all aspects of their career with a label or a manager), it's possible an artist may have to repay these costs through money earned touring, from merchandise and even from songwriting royalties.

With enough notice to the artist, a label can cancel a contract or elect to not pick up options for additional albums. Alternatively, labels have been known to hold artists to the full duration of their contracts (up to 7 years), even though it's not actively promoting the artist or funding albums. For this reason, many contracts have a "key man clause," which allows artists to re-negotiate or get out of contracts if the person who signed them leaves the company and the artist is left with no champion at the label. The artist should also try to secure a "positive release commitment," which allows artists to break the deal if the company hasn't released their material in a specified amount of time.

Having said this, a record company that believes in an artist and puts its full resources behind a promotion campaign can make an artist's career skyrocket. Labels can effectively manufacture your product, promote your music to radio and media, distribute your music, manage sales, and create business in many regions and countries for an artist. They will take large percentages for this, but the artist/band can earn money from CD and merchandise sales (once all expenses have been repaid for the production and promotion of the music/videos), and significantly build their brand. With the earning power usually 3:1 in favour of the record label, though, you're gambling that the company's reach, infrastructure and commitment will outweigh the rights you have to forfeit, and still earn you more money and develop more of a market than you could have as an independent.

Trackers, Pluggers, Publicists

Bear in mind that independent artists have the ability to seek grant money from FACTOR, The Canada Council for the Arts/Conseil des arts du Canada, provincial grants agencies and municipal grants agencies to fund their projects. They can also manufacture their own records, sign independent distribution deals and hire other industry people.

Radio Trackers: Can be hired to promote your single to radio. Good trackers are on a first-name basis with all the major music directors in your market, and can get airplay for their artists. They provide tracking sheets that chart the momentum of the single, and this can be helpful for follow-up efforts. When a song is getting regular airplay in a town, radio interviews can be arranged, and gigs organized to support the song and build the fan base. Radio campaigns usually last 2 to 3 months, and cost several hundred dollars per week.

Song Pluggers: Like the traditional song pluggers associated with publishing companies, independent pluggers can be hired to pitch your songs to publishers, artists, producers and music directors. They will also provide documentation of calls made and meetings held. They charge a flat fee per week or a percentage of future royalties if a song gets placed, or both.

Publicists and Public Relations Companies: Can be hired for a promotional campaign to try to get exposure in print, online, at events and on TV. They generally charge a weekly fee and will also give reports of their work. Publicists can be very helpful in breaking into new markets and raising your profile, especially if there is any kind of a newsworthy story attached to the release of your album, tour, etc.

As you can see, independent artists can get access to most of the main functions a record company can offer, but without giving away too many rights. However, all these tasks cost money (upfront), and can be expensive. Some artists report that it can be very worthwhile to be with a label for a few years to build a brand, and then manage your career independently after that.

Sync Licences

A master recording is the final, ready-for-market recording used for manufacturing. It has also come to take on a legal significance for the person(s) who possess ownership rights to this specific recording. The owner of a master recording is usually the person or group who funded the project, and they will be eligible to earn money from its use in TV and film, through signing a sync (synchronization to film/video) licence. Sync licences are always negotiated on an individual basis with the music user, and fees are generally paid one time only. Please note that the sync fee has nothing to do with the royalties earned through the actual broadcast of the recording on radio, TV, etc.

Songwriters also earn money from sync licenses, but there are two separate pots of money, for ownership of the master recording (which may include the songwriter) and for ownership of the song itself. It's common, for instance, for songwriters to sign a sync licence for a song they wrote, while a separate sync licence goes to the person who owns the master recording of the song or a cover version of the same song.

There is no set tariff for sync licences. It is up to individuals to negotiate the best deal they can. A big hit may command a sync fee in the neighbourhood of $100,000, while an unknown may get $500. It depends on the prominence of the song in the film, video or game and the prominence of the artist. The bigger the artist, the bigger the licence fee.

Neighbouring Rights

In Canada, Re:Sound Music Licensing Company is a non-profit umbrella collective representing performers and makers of sound recordings. They define the rights as follows: "Neighbouring rights are the rights of performers and makers of sound recordings to be paid fairly for the broadcast and public performance of their works. The maker of a sound recording is defined in the Copyright Act as the person who makes arrangements for the first fixation of the sounds, including entering into contracts with performers, and making financial and technical arrangements." Royalties are paid out by music users and broadcasters to sound recording makers, and tariffs are set out by the Copyright Board.

The Private Copying Levy was introduced (in 1999) to offset lost revenues due to the rampant copying of music by the public. The Canadian Private Copying Collective (CPCC) is the agency responsible for collecting and distributing royalties to singers, songwriters, musicians, publishers and record companies. According to the CPCC, "a blank CD costs in the range of 50 cents. Of that, 29 cents is collected for singers and songwriters and other rights holders in music. This royalty is called the private copying levy and it provides compensation to creators for private copies that are made of their music without authorization."

Re:Sound administers neighbouring rights collected from music users and from the Private Copying Levy, and has five member groups that form its collective:

Re:Sound Member Collectives Representing Sound Recording Makers' Rights

CONNECT (Connect Music Licensing) and SOPROQ (la société gestion collective des droits des producteurs de phonogrammes et de vidéogrammes du Québec) are the two Canadian organizations that collect and deliver royalties to makers of sound recordings (the owners of master recordings) through their broadcast and reproduction.

Re:Sound Member Collectives Representing Performers

MROC (Musicians Rights Organizations of Canada) is a federal non-profit organization that collects and distributes royalties to musicians and vocalists from both neighbouring rights and the private copying levy. MROC is primarily focused on compensating recording musicians (who must sign up on with MROC and declare the recordings they performed on).

RACS (the ACTRA Recording Artist Collective Society) and ARTISTI (La société de gestion collective de l'Union des Artistes) are English and French organizations that represent unionized actors' interests in collecting and distributing neighbouring and private copying rights.

Mechanical Rights

Mechanical rights are attributed to songwriters and publishers who own the intellectual property rights of a song; a fee to record and make the song commercially available must be paid to the owners. In Canada, no CD manufacturer can process an album until all necessary licences for Mechanical Rights have been procured and produced. If you're an artist who needs to acquire permission to record a cover song, you contact either the CMRRA (Canadian Musical Reproduction Rights Agency Ltd.) or SODRAC (Society for Reproduction Rights of Authors, Composers and Music Publishers in Canada), and pay a fee based on projected usage. As a songwriter, you can register your (recorded) works with one of these agencies so if a third party wants to record your song, you will receive the mechanical royalties owed.

From The Trenches

I can attest to the fact you want to do this very early in the process of recording an album. When I recorded an album of all Beatles tunes, I had no problem getting licences from the CMRRA for all songs except one. The CMRRA was able to gain access to the Lennon-McCartney catalogue, but a George Harrison song was not represented by the CMRRA (and they had assumed it was). So I didn't find out until a week or two before the manufacturing date that I didn't have permission for one song. Thankfully, I was able to locate the song's U.S publisher and they were quick to help out, but this was pure luck. If I hadn't begun the process of acquiring licences months in advance, I would have missed having product ready for the CD release.

Performing Rights - SOCAN

In Canada, SOCAN is the only Performing Rights Organization (PRO). SOCAN defines performing rights as follows: "It is the right to perform musical works in public or to communicate them to the public by telecommunication. SOCAN's members have assigned this right to SOCAN to administer (i.e. collect and distribute royalties) on their behalf. Tariffs for performing rights are set by the Copyright Board of Canada. SOCAN fees generally work out to mere fractions of a penny per song."

The fees SOCAN refers to are for licences that businesses must acquire in order to play music in public, whether it be live or recorded music. A licence from SOCAN grants businesses blanket permission from all songwriters and publishers to play any music they like under the assumption that music creation is directly benefitting the business. The purchase of recorded music allows it to be played only in private and non-business settings and a licence is required for public use. Similarly, a band hired to play in a public setting may be paid by a business for its performance, but the business also has to pay licence fees to SOCAN to compensate creators for the use of their work.

Membership to SOCAN is free, but music creators must meet the following criteria:

- Be a music composer, songwriter, or lyricist.
- Have created a musical work or part of a musical work that has been: published by a music publisher; recorded; or performed (or will be) in a public forum (i.e. radio, television, film, live performance, satellite radio, ringtone or Internet) subject to licensing by SOCAN.

As a general rule, members should register their works whenever a commercial recording of a song has been made, and be sure to list all co-writers (and the percentage each one is entitled to). SOCAN does not receive any recordings or written documentation (fixations) of the music itself, but they will catalogue your titles and all pertinent information that will allow you to receive royalty payment.

SOCAN collects and manages huge amounts of information from a wide variety of sources, so royalty payment is never received right away. In most cases, payment is made 3 quarters (9 months) after performance.

When becoming a member of SOCAN, songwriters must also select which American Performing Rights Organization they wish to join as a sort of U.S affiliate, of which there are three: ASCAP, BMI and SESAC. Before deciding which PRO to go with, assess each one's strengths and weaknesses relative to your needs – a little homework will help you decide which one to select. This being said, most songwriters feel they are similar enough in nature that there is little danger in making a gravely wrong decision.

The licence fees gathered by SOCAN go toward operating costs (14%) and the rest goes toward royalty distribution. In order to receive payment through SOCAN, your work has to generate income from one of the following:

- Internet
- Concerts
- Radio
- Satellite Radio
- Television and Cable

- Cinema
- Ringtones
- International Broadcast
- Private Copying

At the moment, all forms of payment from the Internet, including streaming services, audio-video services, Youtube, and websites are very low (although ringtones can prove lucrative for some people). I'm certain this will be more fairly regulated in the future, but for now, the two main ways songwriters and publishers can get paid are from concert performance and broadcast.

Concert Performance

In addition to all forms of broadcast, SOCAN will pay royalties when your songs are performed live in concert. Royalties are determined by SOCAN's distribution rules for concert performances, and in most cases, the presenter needs to have paid a licence fee (most venues and presenters who regularly stage concerts are licensed by SOCAN). For shows in clubs and bars, a minimum cover or ticket price (as stipulated by SOCAN) must be in effect. SOCAN considers this a demonstration of the fact the public is there to hear your music.

In order to file for royalties, members are required to submit a Notification of Live Music Performance (NLMP) form that provides details about their performance. These forms are available online or at any SOCAN office. As well, proof of performance is required in order to submit an NLMP form, like a ticket stub, newspaper clipping, program, contract or letter/email from the promoter – something to prove that the performance took place and the entry fee was charged. Members have up to one year after a performance to submit this information to SOCAN.

When completing the NLMP, you will be asked to include all songs performed, including covers. Be sure to include them so other songwriters get paid, too.

Broadcast Performance

Broadcast performance includes radio, satellite radio, TV, video and film. In general, royalties are paid when SOCAN receives notification your work has been broadcast. There is an elaborate system in place to determine the tariff you will get paid based on song duration, number of performances and a credit system (for up-to-the-minute details on royalty collection and distribution visit SOCAN's website). Here's a brief rundown on avenues for broadcast performance:

Radio and Pay Audio

Census Radio: Major market commercial stations are monitored via census that is said to report up to 96% of all performances. To get paid by census radio, a work must be registered with Nielsen BDS, the organization that monitors performance using a patented digital pattern recognition technology, and reports to SOCAN and media publications like Billboard and Jam!. This is where the big money is.

Survey Radio: Smaller market commercial radio stations not monitored by BDS technology report programming to SOCAN on a quarterly basis. It should be noted, however, that reporting represents only a sample of programming, based on about 28 days of programming per station per year. These include community radio stations and generally pay less than BDS-monitored stations.

CBC/Radio-Canada: All CBC radio performances are paid from a dedicated CBC pool. Network and regional CBC radio performances are tracked on a census basis, while local CBC radio performances are sampled across the country and weighted according to the population in each locality.

Pay Audio: Digital pay audio service providers allow satellite and cable television subscribers to access commercial-free, announcer-free, digital sound quality, pre-packaged music. Pay audio performances are paid from a sample of programming information, consisting of 21 days each distribution period. The programming information is given to SOCAN by the pay audio service providers.

Satellite Radio: Satellite radio royalties are distributed from the satellite radio pool and are based on a sample of programming information for the last 7 days of each month for each satellite channel. These performance logs are reported by the satellite providers transmitting in Canada.

Internet: SOCAN licenses a number of Internet music users, including music streaming (audio and video), YouTube, simulcasting of terrestrial radio, webcasting, karaoke, and video games, and are in negotiation to license many more services, such as online concerts.

Payments are based on information received from the licensed Internet services for their online music usage during each distribution period.

Television and Film

With respect to TV, SOCAN states: "SOCAN distributes royalties for all broadcast (terrestrial) and non-broadcast (cable & specialty) television in Canada. All money received from the Broadcast TV stations and Cable stations is placed into two separate pools; the Broadcast TV Pool and Non-Broadcast (Cable) Pool. In order to distribute on these pools, SOCAN receives domestic programming information from Tribune Media Services (TMS), a company that tracks content that airs on TV around the world, and matches it to cue sheet information in SOCAN's database."

As a songwriter, you need to ensure that whenever your music appears on a TV show or in a film, there is a cue sheet completed by the producer that credits your work. The cue sheet will be used by TMS to track and disburse royalties. For both TV and Cinema (movies shown in cinemas across Canada), payment is once again based on a number of factors, like duration, time of day, "station weight" (how prominent the station is) and how your music is used, including:

- Theme music (both opening and closing) – 100%.
- Feature/source music – 100%.
- Concert feature music – 200%.
- Background/score music – 60%.
- Logo music – 5%.

Writing for film and television is a little different than having a song placed in a show. In general, composers receive a fee for service (negotiated independently), and receive performance royalties when the work goes to air. On larger films, there may be a music director to work with, and on other projects the director or producer will be the person you report to. In any event, it's best to get as direct a line of communication as possible to the person with authority to make decisions, and to have a detailed discussion with this person before work begins. Communication is key in making the best use of your time and minimizing the amount of work that has to be re-done because of a lack of clarity. Eliminate middlemen wherever possible.

For those interested in writing for film, TV, video and games, the Screen Composers Guild of Canada represents screen composers' interests. The organization has sample contracts and recommended fee structures on its website.

Libraries

A relatively recent phenomenon is the Music Library. Music libraries function like music publishers, providing material to TV, film, video and gaming companies, advertising agencies, online businesses and photographers. Their catalogues comprise unsigned works – musical compositions that are not the property of any publisher, and for which the composer/songwriter has full ownership of the song itself and the master recording.

The company TAXI, which describes itself as the world's biggest A&R company, is one such library, but with a twist. For various levels of fees, you can become a member of TAXI and receive notifications from diverse clients who are looking for specific types of material. There is an extremely wide range of style and content represented in these listings, and if you think you have a work that sounds like a match for a specific listing, you can submit your work (for a fee).

In many cases, the clients are other music libraries, and writers can get to know the individual companies and develop relationships with them once a placement has gotten you in the door. From then on, you can submit music directly to these companies and avoid any fees. In fact, most libraries now allow you to submit your music digitally, without introduction.

Most music libraries will not try to make you sign your publishing rights over exclusively. In most cases, the writers retain all rights they had for the original work. However, any placements generated by the music library are split 50/50. One technique some companies use to manage this is to rename the works to keep them separate. This requires advising SOCAN of the new title (usually done by the library), so they can pay both parties as writer and publisher. Otherwise, writers receive royalty statements and cheques directly from the library (For instance, if your song is called "I Love You", the library may re-title it "I Really Love You" in their catalogue. When the former is flagged for royalty payment by a PRO, it goes to you. When the latter is flagged, payment is split with the library, who receive the Publisher portion).

When creating mixes and stems to submit, it's highly advisable to make alternative versions that can be used by the client for various purposes. For instance, if the song has a vocal track, there should always be a mix without the vocal. Other mixes might feature acoustic instruments only; just drums and bass; or just a solo instrument. It's also good to make short mixes (10 seconds, 30 seconds, 1 minute); songs with clear endings are preferred over fadeouts.

For artists looking to place their songs, or even instrumental tracks from recordings, in films, TV, etc., music libraries can be a good way in. And for writers who have written cues for theatre that will never again see the light of day, music libraries can be a great way to find new homes for good work.

Theatre

When writing music for theatre, all writing fees are negotiated individually, and most will include timelines where certain work must be delivered. Whenever writing for a specific project with specific needs, it's best to have a detailed discussion with the person with most authority (usually the director) to gain a shared understanding of issues like style, entries, durations and the role of each cue in terms of emotion and dynamics (is it underscoring, an accent, a theme associated with a character?).

Some projects, like musicals, require many songs to be written. Other projects may need one or two, and still others no songs at all. Composers need to make it clear that they have full ownership of all their work (unless it's otherwise agreed to share copyright, and I don't know why anyone would unless it's with a playwright who is also lyricist). This is important so you're free to exploit the songs you wrote for the show, or if you want to recycle cues for other shows (not generally advisable for your reputation) or with a music library.

If writing a musical, it's a good idea to work with the playwright to see if a partnership can be struck, which, in most cases, is only fair. This will allow you to also collect royalties from box office, 10% of which usually goes to the creator of the show (which would be split with the playwright). When your show goes up in an "A" house (the larger theatres in major centres), this can represent a fair chunk of cash (and "B" houses are pretty good, too).

Commission

Writing on commission is similar to Theatre. It's paramount that the work satisfies the specific needs of the client, and the focus, boundaries and tone of the proposed work should be nailed down before writing starts. When writing lyrics, it's especially important to zone in on precise key words, phrases and ideas, and to the deliver the client's message above all else.

Commissions usually involve a fee for service and the possibility of performance, sync and mechanical royalties.

Get a Lawyer

Publishing deals, sync deals, record deals and most music industry deals can be daunting and laced with unfamiliar jargon and hidden clauses. It's well worth the (possibly exorbitant) fees a good entertainment lawyer will charge you to have any major deal reviewed before you sign it. They may recommend changes and even negotiate some of them for you, and some of these changes can make a big difference, especially a few years down the road when it may be time to renegotiate or leave the deal.

Beyond that, entertainment lawyers may be able to get your music into the hands of a label, manager or artist. You may pay for this service in either a one-time fee or in a percentage of royalties, but it can be a good investment if it leads to a positive career move.

But most importantly, and I need to say it again: Never sign an important deal without getting legal advice. Ever.

Victoria's Secrets

Take Responsibility. Are you an artist who doesn't have a record label? Are you a songwriter with no publisher? Is nobody jumping to sign you at the moment? Don't wait for a saviour to come along and start your career, then. Start it yourself. Build your own fan base. Use social media. Network like crazy. Pitch your own songs. Make up a fake name and email address and be your own manager, so you look professional. Ultimately, you need to take responsibility for your own career ... get the train moving, and once it's moving, other people are going to want to jump on board.

Find Your Believer. When deciding who to work with as a publisher, a record label, a manager, or anything of that sort, hold out until you find someone who passionately believes in you. You'll need that person who will fight for you and won't take no for an answer. This business is tough, and success requires time, risk and investment ... so you need someone who is going to hang in there with you through the hard times long enough to get you to the good times.

Network, Network, Network. There are 3 elements for a successful music career: talent, luck and relationships. Don't forget about the relationships part. It's crucial! Half of my time as a professional songwriter is spent writing or in the studio. The other half is spent going out to shows to see and meet new people, supporting my co-writers when they play out somewhere, going to "number one" parties or Music Row BBQ parties to shake hands and network with other music business people, going to songwriting festivals to make new connections, and going to awards shows/industry events. You can write the next hit for Carrie Underwood, but if you don't know someone who knows Carrie Underwood, Carrie is never going to hear it.

A Brief History of the Craft

Early Songwriters

Anthropologists have found evidence of musical instruments and singing and dancing in most cultures around the world from before recorded history. Unfortunately, most of the music itself is lost to us, but it appears that songs have accompanied work life and other sacred and secular aspects of human existence as far back as we can see.

As songwriters and music makers, we're part of a lineage that has served humankind for centuries, and it can be worthwhile to pause and take stock of our larger role in society. Writing music to be performed at community events like weddings, festivals and funerals is an important function, and the ability to touch people with our work can be healing, motivational and transformative. Music's power to unite has been witnessed throughout history in temples, on battlefields, in celebration and in ceremony, and its influence on the individual has been known to foster change and even save lives.

In Western culture, songwriting started to emerge as an individual art (as opposed to a communal art) after the Roman Empire, in what is now France, during the medieval era (between 5th-15th centuries).

In the Early Middle Ages, Goliards were a group of secular singer-songwriters who were execrated by the church for their obscene and heretical songs about drinking and debauchery (predating Bohemians and punk rockers by a few centuries). Back then, the practice of "primogeniture" was prevalent, whereby the rights of inheritance and other privileges were bestowed upon the eldest son in the family, leaving the other sons to find another means to support themselves (and of course, women's futures were barely considered relevant, and were entirely tied to men's). As a result, many young men sought to gain entry to the priesthood or to a university, which were closely linked in the day.

Many who embarked on academic or clerical careers had little affinity with such a lifestyle, drawn, as they were, to the hopes of a job more than a calling. They also had a difficult time acquiring positions because of the abundance of other like-minded individuals, and this led to resentment, cynicism and a spirit of subversion.

Consequently, these over-educated, under-motivated and under-employed young men adopted lives focused on carnal pleasure and excess, and used satire to undermine the church and its activities from within its ranks. A famous example from this period is Carmina Burana – a work by Carl Orff that sets 24 medieval poems to his music.

All the while, another group of musicians and entertainers was travelling across Europe. "Les Jongleurs" were the originators of "la chanson de geste," writing and singing about the great battles of the day, heroism, social and community issues, the court, romance and the Crusades. Les Jongleurs were often associated with the court of a king or nobleman, and were sometimes sent to entertain other courts as a gesture of goodwill or to spy on rival courts.

In addition to writing, singing and performing songs on a variety of instruments, les Jongleurs were also skilled in juggling, acrobatics, fire eating, dancing, conjuring, poetry, buffoonery and animal training. There are also accounts of Jongleurs being employed as night watchmen and trumpeters in battle.

As time went on, a divide emerged in the courts between Minstrels, another term for the more broadly skilled Jongleurs, and the new arrivals called Les Troubadours. Les Troubadours were seen by the nobility as more fashionable and sophisticated, and they became more specialized as actors, musicians and entertainers.

The replacement of Minstrels by the cooler, hipper Troubadours forced the Minstrels to become nomadic, hence the term "wandering minstrels." Minstrels took to the countryside, performing at fairs and festivals, and also moved from the courts to the cities, professionalizing and forming the first artistic guild in Paris in 1321.

During this time, the church continued to hire musicians, but the music remained liturgical, based on monody (Gregorian chant), with polyphony only slowly starting to develop.

Right up until the time of composers like Haydn and Mozart, the aristocracy remained important patrons of music. Haydn had a dream gig as Kapellmeister for the Esterhazy family. Bach and Handel also were Kapellmeisters to noblemen and affiliated with the church. Unfortunately, Mozart never landed a great patron, and had to eke out his living as a freelance composer. Reliance on the nobility started to change with the rise of composers like Beethoven and Mendelssohn, who were two of the first successful commercial musicians. Like indie artists today, they found sponsors and organized concerts of their own music, sometimes with local orchestras as partners.

If we look to today's music scene, we can see some parallels. The aristocracy is still supporting musicians, as evidenced by the large donations and sponsorships the wealthiest families often give to their local orchestras and musical events. And with the move toward globalization, corporations have replaced the nobility as funders of the arts, donating to events ranging from music tours and TV specials to music camps and artist retreats.

It could also be argued that the university (with funding from federal and provincial budgets in Canada) plays something of a sponsorship role as well, providing employment for composers and performers, furnishing a living wage and developing the next generation of musicians.

The church is still an employer of musicians, and minstrels are still going strong, whether as buskers at the local level, or as travelling musicians of all stripes.

African American Music

The Middle Ages were followed by the Early Modern Period, when routes to North America and the East were discovered, and globalization began. In the late 16th century, Europeans started to colonize

North America, and in 1619, a Dutch ship brought the first Africans, who were forced to come to the New World as slaves.

Based in the call and response of African work songs, the music created in the cotton fields and on the rivers of the Southern U.S. became a creative outlet for the fear, anger and frustration of the African American experience. These songs led to the first "Negro Spirituals", and later to Gospel and the Blues. Such songs helped the people ease their burdens, share their pain and even evade their captors. In chronicles of the Underground Railroad, certain songs were used to communicate important messages to fleeing slaves (i.e. Wade in the Water was sung to alert people of slave-catchers in the area and to avoid trace by walking in the water), and to send signals of when to hide and when it was all clear.

Blues and Gospel evolved, leading to Ragtime, Jazz and such other forms of popular music such as Rock 'n' Roll, Country and Folk. Chicago, St. Louis, Memphis and Kansas City were important cities where the Blues developed in distinctive ways, and the influence of the Blues can still be heard in the scale, phrasing, harmony and attitude of much of today's music.

Tin Pan Alley

Fast forward a few years to the first real hub for songwriters – Tin Pan Alley. This is the name given to the area in Manhattan on West 28th Street between Fifth and Sixth Avenues that housed a concentrated group of songwriters and publishers who controlled popular music in the late 19th century and early 20th century. Although the story behind the name is unknown, it is supposedly an allusion to the din created by so many pianos banging out songs at the same time (akin to the sound of hitting tin pans). Whatever the origins, it was a nickname that came to refer to the American songwriting business.

With the completion of the railroad in the 1860s, performers began travelling the country, and Vaudeville stars would come to Tin Pan Alley to listen to new songs for their shows. The more famous stars were given free copies, or were even paid to sing them, but most had to pay to sing the songs. In this pre-radio era, publishers (who published printed music) worked hard to get well-known performers to bring their songs to the public so that amateur singers and ensembles would buy the sheet music.

Broadway flourished with the steady stream of music Tin Pan Alley provided. Curiously, it was the simultaneous arrival of Jews fleeing persecution in Europe (Irving Berlin, the Gershwins, Al Jolson, Harold Arlen) and the emigration of African Americans from the South that produced the Tin Pan Alley sound. White, often Jewish, songwriters "borrowed" from the African American music they were hearing (Ragtime, Jazz), and created what is often termed The Great American Songbook. Famous Tin Pan Alley writers include: Berlin, Arlen, Hoagy Carmichael, George & Ira Gershwin, Scott Joplin, Johnny Mercer, Jerome Kern, Cole Porter and Harry Warren.

Songwriters who worked on Tin Pan Alley, usually on staff with a publisher who was also in the same building, were treated better than songwriters who came from out of town. When songwriters came to

Tin Pan Alley trying to peddle their wares, publishers would sometimes add the name of a staff writer to songs they took in order to bring in more royalties for the company; or purchase all rights to the song for a flat fee and name someone else (from the company) as the songwriter.

Some songwriters, like Berlin, formed their own publishing companies, and as the music business took on more power, Tin Pin Alley became politically active, creating ASCAP in 1891, and contributing to the war effort. Songs like Over There bolstered troops and families alike during WWI, and a vast array of songs were also written to maintain morale during WWII.

Tin Pan Alley created "song pluggers" to promote the sale of sheet music. Pluggers would demo new songs in music stores (many had a resident music plugger) or at special events. Some travelled across the country to perform in department stores, bringing new music to the buying public. However, their role changed as the business shifted, and publishing no longer referred exclusively or predominantly to printed music.

With the advent of commercial radio and the phonograph in the U.S during the 1920s, Tin Pan Alley started to wane. Records replaced sheet music as the driving force of Pop music.

The Brill Building

By the end of WWII, the Brill Building had become the new hub for the music industry. Just uptown from Tin Pan Alley, the Brill Building became a one-stop-shop for publishers, songwriters, labels, producers, song pluggers, publicists and radio promoters.

In the early days, the Brill Building supplied the famous Big Band leaders of the day – Benny Goodman, Glenn Miller, Jimmy Dorsey and Tommy Dorsey – with a steady diet of material. As the Big Bands faded away, teams of songwriters holed up in offices writing songs for Pop moguls like promoter Don Kirschner, who also managed the Monkees and the Archies.

The focus was on writing hits, mostly for a teenage audience, and getting them into the pipeline supplying American pop music. Publishers would send song pluggers to visit popular artists and bands to persuade them to record their songs, and to radio stations to play them. The Brill Building's days were numbered, however, when the Beatles and Bob Dylan arrived on the scene, and artists started recording their own material.

The Brill Building spawned a host of famous songwriting teams – Burt Bacharach and Hal David, Gerry Goffin and Carole King, Tommy Boyce and Bobby Hart, Jerry Lieber and Mike Stoller, and Barry Mann and Cynthia Weill – as well as writers who also had successful careers as artists – King, Neil Sedaka, Paul Simon, Andy Kim and Neil Diamond.

Motown, Nashville and Other Scenes

Detroit, aka the Motor City, was the birthplace of Motown, a record label started and run by Berry Gordy. During the 1960s, Motown brought African American music into the mainstream, combining Soul and Pop to create huge stars like Diana Ross and the Supremes, The Four Tops, The Jackson 5, Stevie Wonder, Marvin Gaye, The Temptations, Gladys Knight and the Pips and Martha and the Vandellas.

During Motown's years in Detroit, the songwriting team of Holland-Dozier-Holland, Smokey Robinson and Gordy himself carved out a unique sound. When the company moved to L.A., Norman Whitfield picked up the mantle and wrote a succession of hits for the label.

Nashville became a music city giant in the 1920s, when it became one of the first cities to have two major radio stations whose signals could broadcast nationally. This gave artists two paying outlets, and the city attracted talent from all over. Recording and publishing industries developed, and the Grand Ole Opry further put the city on the map. In the 1950s, the first major music businesses started appearing on Music Row, and producers like Owen Bradley and Chet Atkins borrowed Pop music recording techniques to refine what was previously Hillbilly music. The first crossover stars, like Elvis Presley, Jim Reeves and Patsy Cline, emerged.

Nashville has long been considered the Songwriting Capital of the World, perhaps even more so today as it is still a place where songwriters write to a large extent for others.

Other hotspots have also appeared to provide short bursts of influence. In the 1960s, Liverpool was known for its "Mersey Beat" (Beatles,

Gerry & the Pacemakers) and London's Carnaby Street was a showcase area for London's Rock and Blues artists, including Cream, Led Zeppelin and Jimi Hendrix. In New York's Greenwich Village and Toronto's Yorkville, the folk scene flourished with the proliferation of coffee houses and other "happenings." Joni Mitchell, Leonard Cohen, Bob Dylan, Joan Baez, Pete Seeger, Judy Collins and Peter, Paul and Mary were some of the artists and songwriters who flourished in this scene. San Francisco's Haight Ashbury was the hub for Hippie music of The Grateful Dead, Jefferson Airplane, The Mamas and the Papas and Janis Joplin.

Since the explosion of Pop music in the 1960s, other music hubs have emerged in North America and around the world, contributing their own special sound and style, as defined by the songwriters and performers linked to these places. Music scenes are thriving in American cities outside of New York and L.A, like New Orleans, Austin, Seattle and Miami. In Canada, Toronto is the largest city and has the most music infrastructure, but St. John's, Halifax,Winnipeg, Edmonton and Vancouver have important scenes as well, and Montréal is the third largest centre of francophone culture in the world. Outside of North America, English-speaking places like the U.K and Australia are still strong,but countries like Iceland, Portugal and South Korea have made major strides due to the internet and globalization, and music from a multitude of non-Western cultures is finding new audiences and gaining influence.

No matter where we live, today's songwriters are part of a long line of minstrels and bards whose songs help shape culture, weave a growing

Coda

Social change and technological advancements have always shaped the way music is made, and will undoubtedly continue to do so with even greater force in the coming years. For the songwriter, subjects that used to be taboo are now mainstream, and moral boundaries are ever widening. At the same time, matters of social justice are front and centre in the minds of artists, and their messages can reach around the world instantly with the press of a button. Music plays a central role in the lives of so many people, and the songwriter remains a key figure who reflects meaning, beauty and humanity back to a distracted public.

As the pace of change accelerates ever and ever faster, I believe that core principles in art that have been passed down through generations will become even more important. These principles are based in the human condition and form the foundation upon which each new church of thought builds its temple. I hope you found many of these principles in the pages of this book, and use these tools as you build your own church and make whatever music wants to get made there.

Bibliography

Blume, Jason. 2004. *Steps to Songwriting Success.* Revised Edition. Billboard Books. United States of America.

Beall, Eric. 2009. *Billboard Guide to Writing and Producing Songs That Sell.* First Edition. Watson-Guptill Publications. United States of America.

Braheny, John. 2006. *The Craft and Business of Songwriting.* Writer's Digest Books. United States of America.

Cameron, Julia. 2002. *The Artist's Way: A Spiritual Path to Path to Higher Creativity.* Los Angeles: Jeremy P. Archer/Perigree.

Carter, Walter. 1997. *The Songwriters Guide to Collaboration.* Revised and Expanded Second Edition. MixBooks. Ann Arbor, Michigan.

Cooper, B. Lee. 1991. *Popular Music Perspectives.* Bowling Green State University Popular Press.

Davis, Sheila. 1998. *Successful Lyric Writing.* Writer's Digest Books. United States of America.

Davis, Sheila. 1996. *The Songwriter's Idea Book.* Writer's Digest Books. United States of America.

Davis, Sheila. 1985. *The Craft of Lyric Writing.* Writer's Digest Books. United States of America.

Gilbert, Elizabeth. 2015. *Big Magic.* Penguin Publishing Group.

Hyland, William G. 1995. *The Song Is Ended.* Oxford University Press, Inc. New York, New York.

Léger, Robert. 2001 *Écrire une chanson, Volume 1.* Québec Amérique. Montreal, Canada.

Faubert, Danièle. Chenart, Mario. 2011. *Écrire une chanson, Volume 2.* Québec Amérique.

Liggett, Mark. Liggett, Cathy. 1985. *The Complete Handbook of Songwriting.* The New American Library of Canada Limited.

Oland, Pamela P. 2001. *The Art Of Writing Great Lyrics.* Allworth Press.

Pattison, Pat. 1995. *Writing Better Lyrics.* Writer's Digest Books. United States of America.

Perricone, Jack. 2000. *Melody In Songwriting.* Berklee Press.

Pressfield, Steven. 2002. *The War of Art.* Black Irish Books.

Rachlin, Harvey. 1977. *The Songwriter's Handbook.* Fitzhenry & Whiteside Limited. Toronto, Canada.

Ricigliano, Daniel A. 1978. *Melody And Harmony in Contemporary Songwriting.* Donato Music Publishing Company. United States of America.

Snider, Bob. 2005. *Bob Snider On Songwriting.* Gaspereau Press Printers & Publishers. Kentville, Nova Scotia.

Sondheim, Stephen. 2011. *Look, I Made a Hat Collected Lyrics (1981-2011) with Attendant Comments, Amplifications, Dogmas, Harangues, Digressions, Anecdotes and Miscellany.* Knopf.

Songwriter's Market. Annual. Writer's Digest Books.

Stolpe, Andrea. 2007. *Popular Lyric Writing.* Berklee Press.

Webb, Jimmy. 1999. *Tunesmith: Inside the Art of Songwriting.* Journey Publishing Company.

About the Author

Robert Walsh is a musician, speaker, author and educator.

Robert has released 6 CDs as an artist, co-written 3 musicals, and his songs and compositions have been heard on stage, radio, television, film, and at commissioned events, performed by himself and others. His work has been nominated for numerous awards, some of which he has taken home. As a singer-songwriter, musician, musical director and producer, Robert has worked with everything from symphony orchestras to big bands to pop artists to folk singers, with many famous artists and many who should be famous.

As an educator, Robert pioneered a popular high school music course in Alberta, and has given workshops and spoken on various aspects of music making and the music industry across Canada in English and French. He authored the book "Bob's Book of Music Theory" (La théorie musicale selon Bob"), and teaches Songwriting at MacEwan University.

www.robertwalsh.ca

70205924R00144

Made in the USA
Middletown, DE
25 September 2019